I0762509

Unstuck: 101 Doorways Leading from the Blank Page to the Last Page is about staying in love with your writing: feeling excited, mischievous, productive, and hopeful—the opposite of being stuck.

Critically acclaimed, award-winning author and beloved teacher Ramona Ausubel offers 101 exercises that promise to welcome you back to the page again and again to reinvigorate your process and help you see your writing through to the end. Full of personal stories and hard-earned wisdom of a veteran writer, *Unstuck* is written in the first person: human to human, writer to writer.

Organized into doorways and keys, *Unstuck* turns problems into possibilities and presents keys to put into use right now, all designed to lead the writer back to the art—not toward an outside idea or formula. With Ausubel's steady, encouraging advice, find your doorway, unlock the lock, and get writing again.

Unstuck

Also by Ramona Ausubel

No One Is Here Except All of Us

A Guide to Being Born: Stories

Sons and Daughters of Ease and Plenty

Awayland: Stories

The Last Animal

Unstuck

101 Doorways
Leading from the
Blank Page
to the Last Page

Ramona Ausubel

Tin House
A zando IMPRINT
NEW YORK

Tin House

Tin House is an imprint of Zando.
zandoprojects.com

First US Edition 2026
Manufacturing by Lake Book Manufacturing
Text design by Beth Steidle
Cover design by Ash Tsai

Library of Congress Cataloging-in-Publication Data is available.

978-1-96310-871-2 (hardcover)
978-1-96310-879-8 (ebook)

10 9 8 7 6 5 4 3 2 1

Manufactured in the United States of America

For my students

Table of Contents

Part 3

Doorways Up: Getting Perspective

Part 4

Doorways Out: Later Drafts and Moving On

Welcome

I would be willing to make a bet: If you polled all the writers in the world and asked whether they felt stuck in their work at that moment, you'd get a very high rate of affirmatives. For a second we are coasting a wave, diving under and feeling the bubbles on our back, and then we're back to stillness. But what if this moment of stillness is a cue to pause and try a new thing? What if stopping, that breath, is necessary and important and *good*? What if the middle of the creative process—after the initial inspiration and long, long before the moment of completion—is a continuous and energetic series of invitations back in? Here's a doorway, and here's a doorway, and here is another. There is so much emphasis in our culture on the two ends of the creative process: the spark of inspiration and the neatly packaged finished product. Rarely do we talk about how to be in and appreciate everything that happens in the middle, when in fact the middle is where most of the actual work is.

Your piece—a novel, a story, a collection, essay, or poem—when it is finished, is richer because it has been seen and reseen, allowed to grow out beyond its original concept, because it contains the energy of the author's sustained curiosity and genuine engagement. It contains the energy of your lived life through the weeks, months, or years you were writing. What if instead of a slog or a sprint to the finish line, you could think of writing as a continual process of discovery?

Recently an MFA student in the program where I teach sheepishly said to me, "I can't write. I know enough now to see how I'll fail." In the same week a friend wrote me an email saying that the COVID pandemic had flipped her process upside down and she still didn't know how to restart. An undergraduate told me that she wanted to try to write a book, but as a first-generation student she didn't think she was "one of the people who gets to do that kind of thing."

Writing is a way to access ourselves and put into words the experience of being alive, to think through a complex idea, to make an argument that might ripple out in all sorts of unknowable ways. If the writer of that argument stops writing, the world lacks that person's idea. If the first-generation student keeps thinking that she is not the kind of person who gets to take her inspiration and make something, the world is missing a crucial story. This is not just about getting unblocked; it is about making sure that good, true, heart-filled work is made and released to the world.

•

Call it writer's block or imposter syndrome. Maybe we're stuck because we find the world difficult and scary (it is), or maybe we are crippled by anxiety over our own abilities and the fear of failure (we are). Every writer in the history of writers has faced the feeling of a brick wall or a steep cliff. Fear is part of art, but it does not have to be the place art ends.

I have written three novels and two collections of short stories. Another way to say this is that I have spent a large part of the last two decades in one state or another of failure and confusion. Stuck. I have been stuck in early stages, when those blank pages feel like an inescapable void. I have felt stuck in the endless middle, where I often look up and wonder when the expert will arrive who knows which path is correct, which decision will lead me home. I have been stuck and afraid in the end, when the world outside begins to look prickly and dangerous for my new art-baby. In every case it feels as if I am surrounded by walls. Sound familiar?

In my decades of writing and teaching I have created (and gathered from other amazing writers) exercises and experiments that I have come to think of as doorways in and through all those seemingly impervious walls. A doorway is a liminal space where we grow, where one being transforms into another, the space between winter and spring, where the wardrobe turns into a magical land.

These are doors to knock on when you are feeling outside of your own writing, overwhelmed by the prospect of this work, or doubtful of your abilities. They are doorways that get you back inside or closer to your work, that will make you excited and curious again, that allow you to write toward the original love of making sentences and paragraphs and stories about the way it feels to be a person alive in the world right now.

•

I don't want to tell you what to write or to make your writing more like mine (or anyone else's). The purpose of this book is to give you ways into your own weird, gorgeous brain and heart, for your work to be more and more itself. To give you ways to start the piece you most want to write right now. To see that piece through the long, windy, wondrous middle. To finish not what you started but what you discovered the story could be.

Because writing time is precious and this is all about *your* voice, the doorways are short—a page or two—and each one turns a problem into a possibility. At the end of each doorway is a key in the form of an immediately usable exercise. The book is organized in four parts: "Doorways In: Beginning"; "Doorways Through: Continuing"; "Doorways Up: Getting Perspective"; and "Doorways Out: Later Drafts and Moving On."

•

A student recently asked, looking at the bookshelf in my office, "How did all these people get from here to there? From words on a screen to bound on the shelf?" I started to give her practical advice about staying in the chair and reading the right novels, but that is only a small part of how a piece of art grows up.

We are not ever just writers—we are also sons and daughters of good parents and disappointing parents and we are partners who need to grab a quart of milk on the way home and parents who crawl into bed with the little ones late at night to admire them when they are still, even though we know we don't have any tiredness to spare. We are students and teachers. We are readers, taking in the universes created by other minds. Our stories and poems and essays are written in and among and because of these moments. A scene is not only a moment on the page that takes place in space and time—the writing of that scene takes place in space and time too. I remember working on an especially dark section of my first novel, *No One Is Here Except All of Us*, in which the character based on my great-grandmother escapes pogroms by fleeing with her children into the Russian wilderness where she survives on tree bark, and it so happened that this writing day took place beside a swimming pool at a Southern California hotel where my father-in-law was staying while he visited us. I spent the morning in the shade surrounded by Disneyland-bound families and I wrote about starvation. You can't see that in the pages, but the energy of that good, easy day provided an opposite to the story from the past and its fictional counterpart. That strange pairing was part of how I powered the writing.

We do not write outside of our lives or in spite of them, but *because* of them. This book is for writers who have made a choice to carve out significant time and those squeezing writing in while a baby sleeps on their chest or during the lunch hour. This is for those of us dictating a story while driving to work. The walls of stuck-ness are easily built. Time is always short; fear is a capable bricklayer; self-doubt and envy can construct a windowless room in seconds. While I love encouragement and good cheer (can you see me waving my pom-poms? I am!), those are not enough to free us. What I believe in, what has worked for me over and over, is a repertoire of small, playful, and unintimidating experiments. Lots of them. A small choice is huge. So often you need a little light, some air, and a handle turns in your hand, you peek through to the next thing, and you're back, you're in, you're running.

This book contains all the skeleton keys to all the secret doors I know, but where you go will be a place entirely undiscovered, all your own. Send me a postcard when you get there.

Part 1

Doorways In: Beginning

DOORWAY #1

Begin Anywhere

There Is No Better Time, No Right Answer

You have this idea for a novel. A young woman disappears in the woods, or a new planet is colonized, or two people fall in love. Ahead of you there are no fewer than one jillion decisions: Are we in 1876? Is the couple driven apart by their hateful fathers? Does the book take place over the course of twenty-four hours or a year? Is it told in first person? And that's only the big stuff. Every page is a string of words picked by you. Every scene is populated, full of characters and places (real or imagined) where every tree, every vase full of dead flowers, every old, tired cat is placed there by *you.*

You cannot, no matter how much you wish, know at the start how this will unfold. Like all the best parts of being alive, it requires you to enter without a map or a promise of success.

I was in such a place when my eldest child was in the fifth grade and it was time to go on tours of middle schools. I had spent the morning staring at a Word document on which I intended to begin a new novel. The document was a white, ominous nothingness. My job was much too big. Defeated, I closed the computer and picked up my kid at his sweet little elementary school, a place that had seen him through the pandemic, that had brought him from a tiny person to a big kid. We drove to a middle school and parked. Nervous eleven-year-olds and their more nervous parents hummed in small groups. Inside, the building felt huge. The echo of sneakers in the concrete stairwells, and halls leading to other halls. How were we here? How was my small person going to be okay in this wilderness? We came around the corner and there was a lit theater marquee at the end of the hall with these words: "BEGIN ANYWHERE.—John Cage." I stood there for a long minute. My child tugged at me. He did not know how to be a middle schooler yet, as he would not know how to be a high schooler a few years later or all the steps to come after. I did not know what this new novel would contain, as I had not known how the three before it would work until I had written through the years and the many drafts. "I'm ready," I said, and we began there, at the anywhere where we stood.

Key

You are here. You are anywhere. Start with a single scene, a single memory, a single question. Set a timer and keep writing for twenty minutes. Whatever you have done at the end of that time, your page is no longer blank, and you have, beautifully, gloriously, begun.

DOORWAY #2

Primordial Slush

The Matter from Which All Life Is Created

What I have come to understand is that you can't start where you intend to end up (i.e., a book that feels like a book) because you have to start three billion years before that. I'm writing fast, following curiosity and questions, writing scenes even if I have no idea where they're going, writing backstory for characters so I can figure out who everyone is, writing place and space. Eventually you want a book-shaped thing, but before that it takes the shape of a freshly bloomed tulip, the back half of a rhinoceros, a mountain stream, a bird's nest. And before that it's a beam of light or a ball of clay. I remember a friend asking how my second novel was going and I said, "It's a swamp monster that oozes around on the floor waiting for me to feed it dead fishes? Is that an answer?"

This was not the creature I wanted. I wanted a unicorn or at least a sturdy, faithful dog. But here is what I now understand: You don't get a dog right away, you have to evolve there. You have to start with a vat of primordial slush, the making of all life, and that slush is not pretty or decipherable. Then something crawls out and maybe it's a tiny little swamp monster. You need that guy. Yes, that draft is super drooly and it's awkward and lumpy and leaves mud all over the place. The swamp monster will grow arms and legs. When you come back to the second draft, he'll be sitting up at a table and you can tie a little checked napkin around his neck and feed him crème brûlée. And when you loop back for a third draft, he'll have grown a lovely coat of fur and now he's looking more like a recognizable animal. A yak, maybe, or one of those Scottish Highland cows with the long red bangs. In draft four you have an apple tree that's about to bloom and in draft six you have a crescent moon and in draft eight you have a wolf and in draft ten you can start to tuck all these eras carefully together between covers and hand it to someone and when they read it, by magic (and months or years of work), the story that you saw in your mind pops open in the mind of that reader and that's when you get to start calling it a book, but by then I hope you trust that it's also still a yak and still a moon, and that your old sloshy swamp guy is in there covered in primordial soup—the energy and possibility of the entire universe dripping from his slimy, squiggly body.

What I'm trying to tell you is that it's going to be so much messier than you can possibly believe. Our job is to trust the mess. To trust the dust storms and the mud bogs and not rush on toward premature order. Order only matters if it contains something real. Sure, you can write a novel that follows a set of very clear rules and expectations, but you will have written a container, not contents. You will have a harness but no dog. Don't skip the mess, because that's where the magic lives.

Do you hear that this is not a quality assessment? Yes, a first draft can be shitty, but it's hard to get very excited about sitting down to write a shitty first draft when quality control is already in the room.

There's a dude in a white coat with a hairnet and a magnifying glass and he's waiting for me to hurry up and take my failures and turn them into candy apples he can sell. If I'm trying to make candy apples, then a beehive is a failure. If I'm trying to write a novel, then a mud bog is a failure. And even if we are welcoming of failure, as we should be, as it is critical to be, I'm sorry but I'm kicking that white coat guy out the fire escape. There is no quality assessment in the primordial slush draft. The universe did not feel inadequate when all it had was an explosion in space from which all life would emerge.

Key

This is not a key you turn once. As you move through your first draft, you must keep going through this doorway over and over. Write the following on a sticky note and put it on your wall: *It's not supposed to make sense yet.*

You might live in the slush for weeks or months or even years. When life begins to crawl out onto land it could happen quickly, a sudden understanding of your project and what it wants to become. Or it might happen slowly, one little toe out in the sunshine, then back underwater.

This is about the intentional, heartfelt creation of energetic, weird, unformed life. Every writer you've ever admired lives here too.

It's not supposed to make sense yet. It's not supposed to be a book yet. I am discovering something still unknown on this earth. Create energy. Repeat.

DOORWAY #3

Writer Physics

Follow the Energy

A story or a poem or an essay has logic, but it's also a living thing. Imagine that a cat walks softly across the black landscape of a burned neighborhood. One valid approach might be to follow the logic: How did this fire start? Who or what was lost? What will happen to the people who used to live here? Those are good questions and you may answer them, but sometimes logic can sideline us on a kind of frontage road next to the story that never seems to merge into the real stuff of it.

Writer physics, which happily does not require a familiarity with the theory of relativity, is the practice of noticing and following the energy in your pages. That cat moves over the ground, and the ground is radiating with everything that was burned. The ash is full of the energetic force of the house, which was full of the energetic force of the ten years (let's say) a family lived inside that space. The baby who was born on the kitchen floor after a labor too quick to get to the hospital; the photo album of great-grandparents in Hungary; a hundred dinners eaten on a simple plate, a shard of which is under one of the cat's paws.

What happens when the family pulls up in a car in front of this changed place? Follow the energy between the people and the plate shards, the memories, the cat. Maybe the cat, afraid and traumatized, jumps at one of the children and scratches her, and the cut gets infected by something in the ash. Maybe the father becomes obsessed with rebuilding a certain room in the house exactly as it was. Maybe the mother returns in secret alone at night and digs through the rubble herself, looking for remains of her old life. Maybe there's a coyote, also scavenging. All of these ideas grow from pressing together two sources of energy: a character and an object, a feeling and another feeling, a character and a tiny moment, a tiny moment and an object. Energy makes energy. Pretty soon that mother is running after the coyote, which has the cat in its jaws. Pretty soon, she's got a jagged piece of wood, once part of her living room wall. Where does the energy go next?

Key

Take a survey of the energetic forces moving through a scene, image, or moment. Close your eyes and try to feel them swirling around. Pick two and press them together, see what happens when the energy of one thing mixes with the energy of another. What changes? What new force is born?

DOORWAY #4

Writer Math

Adding Pages to Get Where You're Going

When I was a graduate student halfway through my MFA in creative writing, I decided I wanted to write a novel, but I had no idea where to start, so I polled my teachers and other writers I knew. "How do you write a novel?" I asked them. Mostly they laughed at me, but one writer said, "Well, you don't start on page one of three hundred." I've thought about this often. He was telling me that I was not about to walk a rational and straight path toward an eventual arrival at my destination. Writing a novel is inside out and upside down and it's dark all the time and what you put on the page first is almost definitely not the beginning.

Because no one could tell me how to proceed, I leaned heavily on numbers. A person who had a document of about two hundred fifty double-spaced pages of a single fictional story could reasonably say that she had a draft of a novel. I had a ten-week quarter ahead of me, so I did the math: Ten pages a day equals fifty pages a week times five weeks equals two hundred fifty pages. In fact it took me six weeks to get to the last page, but otherwise I did exactly that, finishing with a manuscript in my hands (it was crazed, but it existed).

Second book: Five pages a day equals twenty-five pages a week equals a hundred pages a month equals a draft in two to three months.

I realize that I am not dazzling you with my complex equations here. But this is writer math, not real math, and these simple, clear numbers have been a huge help to me, over and over. I think of the people I've been in workshops with who were dizzyingly talented but wrote only when they had a deadline. They wrote great, amazing stories when someone said, "You need to hand us numbered pages in three weeks." Numbers can be a scaffold or a ladder or a place to lean.

Key

Start by thinking about where you want to end up. Maybe it's a full draft of a novel or a memoir. Maybe it's several short stories or a series of prose poems. Next, consider a timeline that would be the right combination of realistic but ambitious. This is not the moment for magical thinking! If you have a stressful full-time job and a new baby, do not pretend that you will complete a draft in two months, because you will only feel disappointed when it doesn't work. Instead, draw lines around a season of writing—three months at a speedy pace, six months at a trot, a year at a gentle jog. Once you have that season, build a ladder of numbers that you can climb to get from where you stand today to where you'll stand at the season's end.

DOORWAY #5

The Half Draft

Not the First or Last Half, but the Foundation

I wrote a super-extra-crazy-fast first draft of my first novel (that writer math was ten pages a day, five days a week, six weeks). I was a graduate student and that kind of mania was possible then. By the time I was ready to start my third novel, I had two kids and a job, and while there was *plenty* of mania, it was not in the form of lots of writing time.

What I had learned was that a first draft, for me, is the place where I find out what a book wants to be. An outline made too early is a cerebral document born from logic rather than magic. The discovery draft is the land where the energetic force, the wildness, originates. It's where I come to understand the beginning, middle, and end of this living thing I'm making. But writing a whole draft of a book is slow going!

Enter the half draft. This is not the first half or the second half, but the foundational half of the novel. Rather than trying to write into every scene and moment, I write rougher, shorter scenes and skip over small parts that I'm not yet tuned into. I'm aiming for maybe a hundred or a hundred fifty pages spanning the beginning, middle, and end. This is so much more than outline. The DNA of the book is here, the scope is here.

The thread count is thinner, but the fabric of the whole is here. And if I write one page a day (so realistic! no mania required!), five days a week, that's a draft in five or six months. If you're reading this in winter, you could be holding that draft while sipping lemonade in the shade of a leafy tree.

Key

Look at your calendar and find a period of time in which you can write consistently for a few months. It doesn't have to be every day (maybe you are a Saturday writer, or you go away from your life for two weeks to write). You can write a double-spaced page of prose in thirty minutes, if you keep typing. This is within your reach. Imagine how good it will feel to hold in your hands a beginning, middle, and end. Imagine what you will discover on the journey. Build in a little margin because someone will get sick and a work project will take longer than expected, et cetera, but once you have found your season to write, put this time on your calendar and keep showing up. And remember that this is a half draft, so it's okay if you need to skip a scene or sketch one in. You have room to breathe.

DOORWAY #6

The Draft Buddy

I'll Send You Mine If You Send Me Yours

Feedback is one of your most useful tools as a writer. Unless you're writing in a journal that is only for you, you need to hear from others to know how the world you made came through.

But not every draft is ready for feedback. If you read the first draft of my first novel, you would have *so many notes*: Characters appear and disappear! The tense changes constantly! Is there a main character? Hard to say! The thing is, I knew these things already and they were not my concern yet. The first draft is a land of mess and magic and curiosity—we're in the primordial slush. Still, writing alone is really hard. Writing alone, especially over a long period of time, can make a person feel a little nuts.

Back when I was writing my first novel, in those crazy first few weeks of writer math and mania, I had something that pinned me to the world: a teacher who had agreed to collect the pages each week as I wrote them, not for feedback but to be a warm set of hands in which to place this emerging world. There's a good chance I would have quit if not for that teacher. Each week I walked into his office with fifty printed pages and he said, "Hey, look at that!" and then I went back into the darkness. My teacher did read the pages, but he was smart enough to know that I did not need feedback at that stage, only encouragement. You and your draft buddy can decide if you even want the other person to read what you wrote, or only receive it.

Maybe you know someone else who's trying to finish a draft of a novel or a memoir or a book of poems. You can swap drafts, handing each other material at the same time or different times. You can send chunks along the way or wait until you have the whole thing.

Feedback is a big ask, but making a soft landing place for a manuscript, with no further expectations, is easy, and it makes all the difference.

Key

Make a list of potential draft buddies. Include friends, coworkers, family members, and others you know who write. Include people you know well and those you met once.

When you look at that list, pay attention to the names that make you feel open and the ones that make you feel nervous. Even if this person won't be reading the manuscript, they will be in your head while you write.

Reach out to the people whose names make you feel open and see if anyone wants to swap drafts.

Set a date or dates. Put them in your calendar with a big, happy exclamation point!

DOORWAY #7

To Change Your Thinking, Change Your View

Outer Perspective, Inner Change

When I'm stuck, I take a walk. It sounds so simple. It *is* so simple, and I can't tell you how many small or big ideas have floated up like gentle little bubbles while I've walked. Puzzles come into focus. Doorways emerge.

It's not only me. Nonstrenuous exercise can make your prefrontal cortex (the part of your brain responsible for decisions and reasoning) go temporarily quiet, allowing your thoughts to drift. Walking lets your critical rule-making brain chill so that creative thinking can take over. More blood moves toward your brain when you move. Walking triggers bilateral stimulation, which engages both hemispheres of your brain. Walking makes you smarter, in the exact way that writers need.

Joyce Carol Oates (who has written approximately four thousand books) goes for a jog every afternoon, as part of her writing day. Darwin looped his "thinking path" while working out the theory of evolution by natural selection.

Movement of other kinds works, too. Get outside. Look at the horizon or the people around you. Let the world open up.

Key

Stand up from your desk, the couch, the kitchen table. Put on a comfortable pair of shoes and walk out your door. I like to walk for forty-five minutes or an hour, but even ten minutes can change your thinking. Plan this into your writing routine. Maybe you start with a walk or take one in the middle of your writing time, or maybe you save it for the end. (In that case, make sure you take notes on your good ideas so that you don't forget them before you sit down to write the next day.)

DOORWAY #8

Mini-Loops

Question, Hypothesis, Evidence, Retort, Echo

Within a whole story there are a thousand smaller stories. Characters, whether in fiction or nonfiction, move through experiences and are transformed, plots are wound tight and then unspooled, and we're used to thinking about the machinery of those things. But meanwhile, we could zoom into the atomic structure, the kind of cellular building of concern and care, and find narrative rise and fall there too.

I was recently working on a story about a young woman who is lonely in her city apartment and her job as a middle school math teacher.

Most days, as she climbs the stairs in her building on her way back home, she runs into a cute guy who works as a chef.

At first, that was all I had. I did not know what the big story would be, so I looked instead for a smaller story, a mini-loop. I looked for a question this woman might have: Will I be lonely always? Answering that question was not my concern just then. That was for the whole story to discover. She'd tossed this question out, and all I needed to look for was one sign or symbol, one hypothesis or guess. In this case, that came with a story development: a mass shooting in a nearby grocery store. So the first hypothesis is: Maybe, yes, sadness grows. But then, a retort or contradiction: The cute guy shows up in the woman's apartment and she realizes that he is a ghost, having died in that shooting. For the first time, she is not alone. In the next moments, we gather evidence in images of both loss and warmth—this impossible being preparing real food in her kitchen when she'd usually eat something from the microwave, for example. These images echo the ways in which sadness has delivered a kind of literal company, that these two forces are linked. That mini-loop gives way to others like it, almost like a wheel that keeps turning through the story: Will I be lonely always? And the hypotheses are some revolving and shifting combination of: Sadness is part of you, and here, too, is company and love. The specifics of the sadness and the love change in volume and nature, and the echoes are differently colored and lit. Sometimes one part feels much larger, sometimes it fades. A story may be one loop turning and turning, or it may be a hundred micro-loops whirling in different directions. In every case, paying attention to the small turnings will always make the big story richer—little questions get tossed into the wind and ideas come back. Questions, hypotheses, evidence, retorts, echoes. Within these are the atoms that make the bigger circle feel complex and whole.

Key

Take note of small or big questions that characters or images are asking. Follow each with a hypothesis in the form of an image, gesture, or decision by a character; then a piece of evidence in the form of another image, gesture, or decision; then a retort. Finally, once you have those four, return to the original hypothesis and change something about it slightly or relight the scene so that the new pieces of information have been incorporated, creating an echo.

Here's how that looked in my story:

- A young woman greets a cute guy in the stairwell. Question: Will I be lonely always?

- The landlady is in the cute guy's apartment, cleaning it out. Hypothesis: Yes, loneliness is here to stay.

- The woman takes the chef's knives. Evidence: There could have been connection, but the possibility was taken away.

- The cute guy, now a ghost, is in the young woman's apartment. Retort: It's complicated, but here is some company.

- The cute guy teaches the young woman to cook a perfect omelet, but as a ghost he can't eat, so she has to consume everything for both of them. Echo: Loneliness is here, but so is connection.

DOORWAY #9

Defamiliarizing the Familiar Through Research

The Stories Behind Everyday Objects

We are surrounded by *stuff.* Each thing in your vicinity was made by a person or a machine, with some purpose. Each thing was invented all at once or evolved over time. There's a story in the object and a story in the people behind it.

Did you know that there is a small hole in the top of every Bic pen cap to prevent people from choking if they swallow the cap? Same goes for Lego minifigure heads.

In ancient China, there was a belief that jade pillows would boost intelligence, and ancient Egyptians believed that evil spirits could enter through your dreams, so people who could afford it slept on pillows made of marble and ivory carved with protective images.

In the sixteenth century a trove of graphite was discovered under a tree in England. It was cut into slivers, which were wrapped in string and sold in the streets. The first pencil! People liked it because it meant less spilled ink. Then, for hundreds of years, pencil marks were erased with balled-up pieces of bread, until a scientist accidentally picked up a blob of rubber next to his bread ball and rubbed it on his paper.

Everything around us is more interesting than we realize. Everything characters use, every piece of an image, can be opened up and rediscovered.

Key

Look around the space you are in (in your life or on the page) and make a short list of things you can see. What's on the shelf, in the fridge, strewn across the grass? Pick one thing and spend fifteen minutes learning about it. Who made it, or who invented the original? Why? How has it changed over time? What are the secret stories contained within? What does the machine look like that makes it? Can you fold one or more threads of this into your piece?

DOORWAY #10

"Yes, And"

Learning from Improv Comedy

If one actor walks onstage claiming that her right foot is on fire and the next actor walks out and says, "I don't think your foot is on fire," the scene reaches a binary disagreement, which isn't all that interesting to watch. If, instead, the second actor walks out, kneels down, and warms his hands over the burning foot, something funny has started to occur. In improv comedy, the principle is always to affirm what has come before, and add to it.

In writing, the principle is not to shut down or distrust your own instincts or ideas. Let's move the burning-foot woman to the page instead of the stage. Because improv comedy works on a bigger, louder scale and I'm writing fiction, I'm going to turn the volume down a bit. The woman is in the kitchen and she drops a match on her shoe, and the laces catch fire. My job is not to argue against this image but to "yes, and" it. She's alone in the house and it's a new house and she's recently moved in after a divorce and none of her stuff has been delivered so it's her, alone, on fire, in an empty kitchen. She kicks the shoe off and dumps a cup of water on it so the immediate danger has passed, but now she's standing over this mess and the mess is all she has. She has no other shoes (that's a "yes, and" to all her belongings being in transit), so after cleaning up, she goes to Target wearing one sneaker and purchases a pair of bright green plastic clogs off the clearance rack because she doesn't have extra money in this new reality. Now, here we are at Target and I want to make use of the potentially awkward situation so let's "yes, and" the scene and here comes one of her children, home sick from school (she didn't even know he was sick because the kids are with their dad, and this makes her profoundly sad), and the kid sees his mom wearing one shoe and carrying a pair of ugly green clogs and they hug and say nothing until Dad comes around the corner.

I don't know what happens next, but I know I'll keep "yes, and-ing" to find out.

Key

It's easy to doubt your ideas or to backpedal when something feels hard or uncertain. Instead, try trusting what you have put down or imagined. Say yes to it, then ask: What else? What might happen as a result of this? What might it lead to?

Not only does this allow you to build, rather than tear down, your work, but it's a reminder to be playful. Improv works because everyone on stage is in on the same project together—the creation of a funny, strange, emergent world. Your work may or may not be funny, but this kind of playfulness serves serious work too.

DOORWAY #11

The Sandwich Rule

Two Normals and a Weird

Down a quiet, oak-lined street where the houses have tidy lawns and Halloween decorations walks a middle-aged woman. She's wearing pleated wool trousers and a navy-blue turtleneck sweater and looks like she's recently gotten her chin-length straight brown hair done. Everything here is normal, or at least it's one kind of normal. In other words, who cares? But as the woman gets closer, we see that she has something on a leash. It's small. Too small to be even the tiniest breed of dog. Is it . . . a rat? In a miniature pink harness bedazzled with rhinestones? Friends, it certainly is.

This is the one-of-these-things-is-not-like-the-other-ones rule. Our brains are excellent at finding patterns and making matches, and there is a certain pleasure in this habit. If the woman had had a groomed poodle, no one would have been surprised, and it would have felt right. But there's no narrative in everything being right all the time. The writer's job is to find the surprise. Sometimes it's a surprise in the events (the butler was the murderer all along!), but you have so many more opportunities to arrest attention (yours, your reader's) and discover new elements of the story than those big plot twists. Sometimes knowing a quirk about a person can entirely change the way you write them, henceforth.

Key

Look for patterns in your characters, your settings, the progression of events. The dad is always quiet and kind, huh? Find one situation where he cannot keep it together. The kitchen in the vacation home the family has checked into is sparkling clean? Put something weird in one of the drawers. Even if you are writing nonfiction, you get to dig through the treasure and muck of the past to find images and details that brighten or offset one another.

You are in control of how strange the strange is. Dad could be quiet and kind except when discussing a previous political administration or a parking ticket or his daughter's mismatched socks. Surprise works on us even when it's slight. Find patterns (in your pages or in your thinking), and throw an anchovy in with the PB&J. I may not want to eat it, but I promise you'll have my attention.

DOORWAY #12

The Black Hole to Which All Other Matter Is Drawn

Finding the Center of Gravity

Every piece of writing has layers. I could ask you what happens (plot), or what the characters want or think they want. We could discuss various themes. But somewhere beneath and between all of that, somewhere at the very deepest center, is what I think of as The Black Hole to Which All Other Matter Is Drawn. The writer Brad Watson said this phrase to a workshop I was in long ago, and it has stayed with me as a central guiding question ever since. It's also the question I ask my workshoppers to articulate at the start of every conversation, and it always reveals so much about what the piece is and what it wants to be.

But what is this black hole? you ask. The black hole is the unending, ever-powerful force that pulls everything else into its orbit. For me, the black hole of *The Great Gatsby* is power as a kind of insatiable hunger. It grows and grows and grows until it eats its own source.

Your black hole might be different. That's why literature is a dynamic thing, felt by each reader in their own way. There is no right or wrong answer to this question, but it's a powerful navigational tool.

I had a clever idea about a Cyclops writing an online dating profile a few years ago. There were obviously going to be some funny moments, but I also wanted this story to mean something. As I wrote, I tried to name the black hole. It was about the dream of being seen, about a character trying out the craziest idea of all: honesty. Everything else in the story is pulled together by that force. All the jokes, all the situations, are in the same orbit.

This is a doorway that I walk through over and over as I write. It's useful in an early draft, but it keeps being useful (and it often keeps changing) as I understand the story better.

Key

For each new story, essay, chapter, or poem, start a document on your computer or a page in your notebook titled "Black Holes." Every so often, revisit this and try to articulate what feels like the very center to you, right now. It may be that there is more than one, which is fine and good (this is your universe and astronomy gets to work exactly the way you want it to!). If you know what's at the center, if you know what the strongest force is, you can feed it with images, scenes, moments, and details. The black hole gets bigger and stronger. The piece itself gets bigger and stronger.

DOORWAY #13

The "What Ifs"

The List That Changes Everything, Every Time

If there is a central tool in my writing practice, this is it.

Whenever I get stuck, whether it's in the first draft or the eleventh, I stop and make a list of "what ifs." I like the list to be long—I aim for twenty-five—so that I really go off and explore the possibilities before coming back to the page. These "what ifs" have to do with character; setting; the inventory of objects in the scene, story, or book; plot; tone; everything.

By way of example, let's imagine that we have a young woman at home who has learned that her mother is dying.

- What if the young woman has recently fallen in love and has a flash of resentment at having to interrupt that happiness?

- What if she was washing the dishes when she got the call, and after the call she looks at her cell phone, then carefully and calmly puts it in the dishwater and walks away?

- What if she opens the refrigerator and starts throwing eggs at the wall?

- What if the mother has always been a furious storm of a woman?
- What if the mother has always been hardly a whisper, someone no one can get to know?
- What if the young woman's three older brothers live in three identical suburban houses and have three identical suburban wives and perfect children and the young woman lives in a little apartment in the city and does not match any set?
- What if the young woman's mother is very poor?
- What if she is very rich?
- What if she lives in a place that is difficult to reach and will take her daughter three days to get to, and that journey is part of the story?

This is not a story I've written and I don't know what happens, but I hope you can see that what I'm trying to do is begin with what I do know or what I want the story to be about and then start looking around the world of this story to see what's possible. In a list I am able to consider what it might feel like if the mother were very rich—maybe she won the lottery and won't share her winnings, or maybe she won the lottery and gave every cent of it to her church or the local animal shelter or the Republican Party. I am watching and listening for what makes electricity in me, in the story. Somewhere in this list I always find the next doorway. And that's all you need: one good detail to wake yourself up.

Some of the items I abandon quickly, some are good ones I haven't yet figured out if I can use in a future project, others are fully implemented. This represents about 20 percent of the length of the first draft. This is a good marker for how much time I spend in this mode of imagining. I get better material when I'm awake to the possibilities.

Key

Open a new document. Make a list of twenty-five "what ifs." These can be story-wide or specific to a scene or moment. It's important to make the list long so that you have a chance to get past the easy ideas. They do not have to be linear, so just because you wrote "What if a lion eats the baby's teddy bear?" that doesn't mean the next line can't be "What if the baby drops the teddy bear in the toilet?"

"What if the story takes place entirely in one dark room?" "What if the man eats ketchup with a spoon when he's sad?" Write things that make very little logical sense but a lot of emotional sense. Write things that feel almost but not quite right. Write things that make you crack up. Write things that nearly break your heart. The list can take up all sorts of territory, from the peculiar to the funny to the gorgeous.

Every time you get stuck in your story, instead of stopping, switch over to the "what if" list and write twenty-five new possibilities. Read it back and see what makes your blood move. Get back to work.

DOORWAY #14

Inventory

Use Your Props Well

When I was writing my first novel, *No One Is Here Except All of Us*, I was working on a scene where the parents announce to their three children that they have decided to give the eldest daughter to her childless aunt and uncle. I knew this would happen in the book, so I had the plot figured out, but I needed the scene to express all the emotion of the moment. My first attempt was a stilted conversation and a lot of "She paused," and "No one knew what to say." The girl's state seemed fairly inexpressible, beyond language. So what did I have? Well, they were sitting around their dinner table in their tiny house in northern Romania and they were eating what they always ate: Mother's homemade cabbage soup. Cabbage soup, I thought, okay. What can we do with cabbage soup? And the next thing I knew, the eldest daughter, who was about to be given away, began to wash her hands in the soup. Here was the elixir of her home, her family, and her hands were pink and hot, and then, in a gesture of understanding, the rest of the family joined in.

Key

Things and what characters do with them speak loudly. Go through your manuscript and underline all the *objects* in a scene or a few scenes. Pretend you are staging the story and need to know what to tell the prop people. Now examine that inventory. Which objects are stagnant, static, not worth your prop budget? Which ones are humming with meaning? Can they matter more, do more? Wherever possible, consider off-label use. All matter has to matter.

DOORWAY #15

Echoes

Each Time We Hear the Thing, It Creates a New Note

When I was in the seventh grade the school cafeteria sold single red roses on Valentine's Day, and because there was absolutely no way anyone at school was going to buy one for me, I sneaked over right before class and bought one for myself. That is image number one of a red rose. A few years later, in high school, my sadly uninspiring boyfriend worked in a flower shop and often brought me the wilting throwaway flowers. That year, my room was full of half-dead roses. Even the exact same thing does not *mean* the same thing to the girl at twelve and the girl at sixteen. I'm constantly revisiting my inventory, revisiting the space in which my characters live, revisiting the way they talk, the way memories shift for them.

Key

Examine your inventory again and pick one thing to bring back. Turn the object around a few times in your mind. What does the world expect it to symbolize? What are some less expected options? How could this thing's meaning change? What note does it sing? How does one new note change the song?

DOORWAY #16

Half as Much Plot, Twice as Much Character

Keep Your Focus on What Matters

Have you ever heard the irritatingly good packing advice to bring half as much stuff and twice as much money as you think you'll need for a trip? You probably won't need the satin shoes *and* the velvet ones, but you'll totally have to buy a twenty-five-dollar sandwich in the airport when your flight is delayed.

Early in the writing process, plot outlining (or even plot imagining) is like packing a suitcase that seems to have no physical limitations. You can throw in thirty side quests involving a lost rhinoceros, plus a part about how the grandmother used to be a pilot, oh, and there's this fascinating thing about the financial architecture of your invented planet and its society, along with backstory about every minor character and seventeen different battles with seventeen different armies.

But then it's time to start writing, and it turns out that the limitless suitcase of plot ideas necessitates hundreds and hundreds of written pages. Every battle needs a lead-up and a reason for the fight, not to mention descriptions of each sword swing and boot kick. The grandmother's aviation career takes three chapters because one time she lost her passport and one time she got food poisoning and one time she met the now-defamed president and he convinced her to invest in a pyramid scheme involving a superfood berry.

What was this novel about again?

Even if you are writing a mystery or a romance, which tend to be more driven by plot than higher-brow literary fiction or narrative nonfiction, you cannot get us to invest if we don't care about the characters. Finding out who they are and what they want drives the story forward. Characters are the holders of plot. We want to know what happens *to them*, not what happens in general. And like a puffy jacket, characters take up space. They are the bulkiest thing you can put in the suitcase, and you need room for them to live and breathe.

Key

Cut half the things on your plot to-do list. Spend twice as much time in moments that matter to characters. Maybe you need one scene of Grandma flying a jet through the night sky because it helps to explain why her granddaughter, the protagonist, drives her old beater to the desert to look at the stars. A single excellent battle scene does more work than six rushed battle scenes. Pick two side quests that really matter to your character—and center your character in those quests—and write them patiently, because you have time to do that now without such a full itinerary.

DOORWAY #17

Sense Immersion

A Meditation for Starting the Writing Day

Over and over again I learn that I know more than I think about a piece of writing, if only I slow down to pay attention.

In a windowless classroom in northern Colorado, twenty writers are told to close our eyes. The visiting writer, Lauren Groff, tells us that her writing day always begins with a meditation. Graduate and undergraduate students, teachers and the library's dean, even a shaggy black service dog, working, all let their eyelids fall. The energy in the room changes. We take three deep breaths in this new quiet. Lauren says, "Place yourself in a scene you want to write. You are going to bring your senses online, one at a time."

Key

Close your eyes.
Breathe deeply and slowly.
Place yourself in a scene you want to write.

First, pay attention only to taste. This might be subtle, something in the air if you were to put your tongue out. Heavy humidity, the toast from breakfast. Take several deep breaths here.

Next, bring in smell. Notice the faraway honeysuckle, car exhaust, a rotting apple on the ground. Take another few breaths, paying attention only to the olfactory realm.

Next, bring in touch. Breathe and feel the air, the temperature, clothes on skin, anything you might be able to reach out and feel.

Next, bring in sound. Rustle of a heavy down jacket, a dog howling, a bus squeaking to a stop. Pay attention to sounds nearby and sounds far away, sounds loud and sounds soft.

Last, bring in sight. Look around this space—what stands out right away? What do you have to squint to see? Is there anything hidden?

What do all those tastes, smells, sounds, and sensory details look like, now that you can see them? Take a few breaths in this fully alive space.

Choose one detail to start with. Open your eyes and start writing.

DOORWAY #18

Twenty Minutes Past Enough

A Last Push to Come Around the Bend

I had a teacher who used to joke that it takes twenty minutes to write a novel. After everyone laughed uncomfortably, he explained that in order to finish a long project, you write for whatever you planned—an hour, two—and right when you think you can't go any further, you set a timer for twenty more minutes. The theory is that we stop when we're intimidated or uncertain, but usually we know more than we realize, and if we push a little further, we come around a bend.

This is a doorway I don't always want to walk through (I'm tired! I've been writing for an hour! I'm stuck, okay??), but it has proved annoyingly effective, over and over. Sometimes it takes me an hour to write the first two hundred words and in that last twenty minutes I cruise through hundreds more.

You're right there, about to see more than you can now. Go a little further. Let what you *do* know or sense be louder than what you do not yet understand.

Key

At the moment you are ready to slam your laptop shut or throw your notebook across the room, stop, breathe, and set a twenty-minute timer (this is your official sign to buy a cute timer of your very own). This stretch can feel like bonus time, this time-outside-of-time. Let it free you to try something not in the plans. Let yourself peer over the edge of the cliff or behind the locked door.

DOORWAY #19

Leave Your Tomorrow Self a Snack

Never Meet a Blank Page Again

Even someone sprinting their fastest sprint cannot write a novel or memoir or collection of poems in a single sitting. We are animals and we need food and sleep, at the very least. The trouble is that writing is full of interruption, and momentum is constantly broken. Even when I'm in the zone, the Monday morning session after the weekend is almost always harder than Friday was. That's all right, because thanks to Friday me, Monday me isn't starting from nothing. There at the bottom of my page is this note: NEXT: *Scene of the girl at the DMV with the squirrel hidden in her pocket.* Or, NEXT: *Mother stuffs her divorce papers in the cavity of a raw chicken and puts it in the oven.*

I think of this as putting a nice cake in the oven for my tomorrow self. Something approachable, welcoming, a way to reenter the day without having to make a decision. It reminds me that care is part of the writing process. Writing is hard work and every gentling gesture means something. Even if my today self might have had a vague notion of what was coming, this clear and confident prompt from my deep-in-the-project self makes all the difference. Thanks, yesterday self. And I'm off.

Key

You've pushed twenty minutes past your stuck place and now it's actually time to stop. Or is it? One more little step . . .

Instead of closing the notebook or computer, write the word *NEXT* at the bottom of the page and jot down your ideas for the next two scenes, ideas, moments, or questions.

DOORWAY #20

Say Yes to Everything That Walks in the Door

On Trusting Your Subconscious and Following Your Nose

A first draft is not about decisions; it's about possibilities. The origin of ideas is mysterious—I've started stories based on a sign on the wall of a museum, based on a very precise feeling of rage, based on an image, based on a "what if." I have had a stray dog walk into a story. Plenty of ghosts have shown up over the years. I've been in a small plane descending over Kenya, in the body of a pregnant girl who believes she's going to give birth to a bird (and, oh, she's knitting three-pronged booties—okay, sure, yes!). These are not places I would have expected to go. This is me with my hands on the keyboard and a big "WELCOME" sign out front. I don't know what's coming in, but I have tea and gin and hot chocolate ready to serve to whatever curious beast or fowl or lightning strike or moon rock might appear.

Somewhere in the midst of writing my latest novel, I was on the phone with my friend Marie-Helene Bertino, and she said, "How's the book?" and I answered, "It takes place in four countries and there are extinct animals and a teen pregnancy and a Neanderthal and dead parents and rich people who keep zebras. It's like a Las Vegas buffet of a novel. There's a chocolate fountain next to the tower of crab legs, and have you seen the ham table?" Marie is a good friend so she laughed, and she is a writer so she knew not to be worried.

I'm not worried about disagreements or paradox at this point. I'm not worried about having too much going on in the novel. Too much is a good sign—it means I'm open. There will be a winnowing, pattern-seeking draft later and some of the creatures and moon rocks will be sent back into the world (with a hug or high five!), but I know for certain that they will leave traces behind.

Key

This doorway is not about what walks in but about saying yes to yourself, to your subconscious and unconscious wisdom. To the parts of you that know before you know. The more you are in the practice of saying yes to everything that walks in the door, the better you get at noticing what's coming, at being in a state of non-resistance to ideas or images that don't yet make sense. It will feel less and less strange to keep your door open and unsuspiciously take in all the grand, bizarre stuff your mind and heart deliver.

You have two options here, in order to be loyal to the "yes." You can immediately incorporate into the piece the image of the baby owl with the broken wing. Whenever possible, I vote for this option because it is the most sincere way of accepting an idea and seeing what it's all about. Sometimes, though, it's not quite time (maybe this owl appears three scenes from now and you don't want to interrupt your flow), in which case you open your "what if" list and write it there. You can serve the owlet a dead mouse on a silver tray while it waits.

DOORWAY #21

Be Yourself

Letting Go of the Story That Isn't Yours

When I finished graduate school, one of my teachers called to tell me that I had won a surprise fellowship with no strings attached. At around the same time, I got a check in the mail—again unexpected—which was the insurance payout for the car accident that had killed my grandmother. Each was for several thousand dollars, but they felt so different. One was a joyous turn of luck, one a strange, dark reward tied to tremendous loss.

My grandmother was a writer and a huge supporter of my work, and when I thought about her, I felt like she was out there encouraging me to take the money and turn it into stories. Go, go, I felt her say.

But I was afraid, and in that fear I came up with an idea for a writing project that felt safe or smart. I decided to write a nonfiction book about what it meant to consider starting a family at that moment on the planet. I could picture a person talking about this subject on NPR. It was a question I really did wonder about (I was twenty-eight, married a couple of years, on the cusp of such a decision myself), and I convinced myself that I could become the person who wanted to and could write this book. My husband quit his job and for nine months we traveled around the world, riding on camels and trains and sketchy buses and walking hundreds of miles through big cities and mountains and the graveyards of our ancestors. All the while I conducted interviews with people about their children, their lives, their worries.

I learned a lot and enjoyed the thinking and talking, but slowly, the realization that this was not really my project grew louder. Mid-trip, while standing in a marigold-filled temple in Jaipur, India, I let myself admit that the problem was not that I was intimidated by the project (all things worth doing are intimidating!), but that it wasn't my work to do.

I felt defeated and stupid. I had wasted my fellowship and let my grandmother down.

We rode on more camels (two-humpers this time) and galloped on horses across the Mongolian steppe. I tried to forgive myself.

When we came home, something unexpected happened. I started to write short stories, and in and through those stories were all those interviews and experiences. I did want to write about the world right then, and what it meant to be alive in it, and to think of the future. I wanted that very, very much, and I was still intimidated, but I was also exactly the right person for the job.

Key

If you are anything like me, this is a peril that keeps popping up. Maybe you too get snagged on expectations and approval all the damn time.

If you find yourself adrift on still waters, having set out upon the great ship *Should*, consider whether it is time to embark on a new project and leave behind the one that isn't yours to do.

Or whether there is a slanted version that incorporates that useful outsider's curiosity with your own bright self. Hemingway wrote all the Hemingway books already—you're off the hook!

Ask yourself, Am I present? Am I trying to be someone else? What about this idea is genuinely interesting to me? Put your best self at the center of the piece. Write toward the questions and curiosities in your own voice.

DOORWAY #22

Invite the Problem In

There Is No Such Thing as a Frictionless Life

Real talk: I knew I would get stuck while writing a book on getting unstuck. I knew, but still.

I had been trucking along, writing for a month with the kind of pleasure that usually comes in too-short waves. It felt good and easy. Then I took a break and went with my family to my mom's house in Santa Fe for Thanksgiving. There were five pies for ten people (the correct ratio), and all was well. Then, while my family undertook the very dangerous task of working on a jigsaw puzzle in the evening, my small dog and my mom's small dog got into a fight about who was allowed to growl at the cat, and in the midst of the tussle, my finger got chomped. Breaking a bone while doing a puzzle with my lapdog is the most me way to be injured. Other people go heli-skiing or cliff diving, but I don't need such wildness! My pinky would need to be in a splint for eight weeks, and I had to take antibiotics for a possible infection.

Every time I tried to type, my giant, purple-taped pinky hit Caps Lock and I was shouting at myself.

Life is full of small or big interruptions. Kids get sick, adults get sick, cars break down, there are aches and joys that overtake our hearts, and dogs fight over cats. Mine was a small interruption, a small problem, but it slowed me to a stop and I felt the sails go slack. I wanted to be back in that efficient machine of writing, but I am not myself a machine.

This doorway is not simply about brushing yourself off and getting back on the horse, though. Surely having children lost me a tremendous number of hours of work, but this infinite experience of care also changed and informed everything I think about the world and everything I have written since my kids were born. Teaching someone to be a person—to fry an egg, write a letter, clean the toilet, end an argument, remember their coat, love something they can't control—is in all my work, even if I'm not writing about parenthood. It is part of the bigness of my own life. To write, all we need is a pen and paper or a keyboard, but we can't do it well without the bigness of life.

I knew I would have to overcome this pinky-sized problem, to learn to type with a giant finger that still hurt, to move through the setback as smoothly as possible. But that wasn't the whole story. To do that would only be to take something that had happened, that was part of my life and my days, and attempt to make it not exist. For a writer, this felt like an essential kind of mistake. I was stuck while thinking about getting you unstuck—how very instructive! What good practice! Being in this moment with my gauzy pinky and my temporarily altered abilities became part of this book. Not because I told you about it but because I welcomed in the truth of the experience. The energy of the frustration and pain every time I hit the A key. The reminder that I'm both sturdy and delicate, present in a moment in my own bright little life, trying to say something that might matter.

Key

You are not a machine. You are a living writer, and this means that your days are full of complication. Even if you are not writing about a single thread of difficulty, that thread is part of the weaving. Virtually every aspect of your livingness could be viewed as an obstacle. What if, instead, you were to welcome it all in? To allow the energy of the difficulty to be part of what you make, for the bigness of your unique life to be the deep well, not the obstacle. Dear illness, injury, new baby, aging parent, heartbreak, dear job. Dear joy, dear confusion. Dear work and effort. Here we are together, in the making.

DOORWAY #23

The Easy Way

Take the Switchbacks, Not the Cliff

We are overthinkers in our family. Any simple task can be made un-simple. I order and return four pairs of shoes in order to find the one. I change the yarn gauge in a knitting project, which necessitates altering the entire pattern. My mom has a letterpressed sign hanging over her desk that reads "Stop! Think! There must be a harder way!" Isn't it strange how attracted we can be to the most difficult path? How we distrust what feels natural and instead aim straight for the sheer rock wall?

I have repeatedly aimed for the wall as a writer. I have been a homing pigeon for The Harder Way a quadrillion dumb times. Somehow, taking the switchbacks instead of scaling the cliff can register in my brain as cheating or as a less serious path. Is it more valuable to struggle hopelessly in a scene I don't understand at all than to write a scene I have a sense of? NO, but I have to remind myself of this often. Of course, it's okay to challenge myself and work in uncertainty. Still, the scene I *kind of* get will teach me something new, will take me to the next turn in the switchback so that I can see something I couldn't before.

I live in Boulder, Colorado, where every third person is about to run an ultramarathon, bike to Utah, or climb a cliff so high they'll have to stop in the middle and sleep there, dangling in the air. People I know and love run near-vertical mountain trails on their lunch breaks. My friend Tim got "a little bit of frostbite" when his winter solo rock climb took ten hours longer than expected. My friend Brett taught me that there is a state common enough to need a name, in which an ice climber gets to the top of a pitch and it's so cold and they are so exhausted that they both vomit and yell uncontrollably: This, dear reader, is the screaming barfies. I don't need to ever experience this. Bless their hearts. They have abs I'll never have.

But here's the thing: I do want to get to the top of the mountain, and I can. For me, this happens not at a run but at a nice, steady walk. I do not own or need crampons or an ice pick. I'll bring snacks and plenty of water and I'll switchback my way. I'll get the same view at the top and my legs will be tired and happy, and none of my toes will have frozen off.

Key

Writing is a long-haul journey. There's no extra credit for ice-climbing your novel. The piece will not be better because you suffered the most. Do what you kind of understand first. Do what feels interesting first. Do what you love and are good at first. Stop to eat some peanuts and appreciate what you've made so far. Stay hydrated. Writing is hard enough at a gentle pace, I promise. Bit by bit, turn by turn, the view gets bigger, the picture comes together, the moment you did not understand at all is lit by the ones you've put down on the page. Now that formerly hard part is the easier one. "Stop! Think! There must be an easier way!"

DOORWAY #24

One-Word Story

Tunneling to the Center, Then Building Outward

One of my core beliefs is that we know more than we think we know. That our instincts are at work even when our conscious mind feels baffled. This is one of several doorways that aim to access that subconscious wisdom, and it comes to me courtesy of the great writer Eileen Myles. It happens in several stages, each of them informative.

Key

First, open the scene, poem, essay, or story on your computer (it will be unwieldy with a full manuscript, so start smaller). Save a new version titled "50%" and look at the page or word count. The first thing you'll do is trim the piece in *half*, keeping what feels necessary and cutting what might be repetitive, extraneous, slightly to the side. Paste the cut sections into another new document titled "Cuts." This is a deep cut and not at all passive. Don't worry—you aren't necessarily cutting these parts forever. Once you've hit that 50 percent mark, pause and take note of what the piece feels like at this stage. Has anything been revealed to be important or unimportant to you? Which cuts cause a feeling of loss and which cuts bring relief?

Now, save a new version again and title it "25%" and again trim the piece by half, saving the cuts in the same document as before. Take note of what stayed and what went. What remains core and what fell to the side; what you don't want to lose and what you are willing to fight for; which lines or words or paragraphs you can let go of like a balloon released into the sky.

Repeat this process until you have only *one word* remaining. One word to guide you. Here you are, having burrowed deep into the work like a cave explorer, and that word is the lantern in your hand, illuminating the dark space around you.

Stay here for a bit and think about this word, what it tells you about your piece. What it asks for.

You are not here to write a one-word story or poem, though. The first half of this exercise is meant to discover what the piece is by defining what it is not. The second half of the exercise is to rebuild the piece with this clearer sense. Take your lantern and shine it on everything you took away to see what belongs. Add lines back, paragraphs, images, until you have everything you want and nothing you don't.

Don't ever delete that "Cuts" document, because there is sometimes hidden wisdom in there, too, that can be useful later on.

DOORWAY #25

Meanwhile, in the Big World

Creating a Backdrop with Politics, History, and Nature

So much of the work of writing narrative is about finding the center of the story for the characters—what they hunger for, the ways in which they hurt themselves and others. A lot of doorways in this book lead in that direction. Sometimes, though, we forget how the bigger world can add complexity or new notes to the music of the story.

Let's say we've got a young man searching for a gift for his father's birthday months after the young man's mother has died. He doesn't have much money, and everything feels cheap or sad. The thing both father and son want is the thing that cannot be had.

If I want the young man's feelings of loss and love to show up without needing to have him say or think, "I'm sad my mom died and I'm sad my dad's partner died and I only have twenty-seven dollars to show him that I love him," I need to find ways for these feelings to echo or reflect back from other directions or in other imagery.

I'm going to put this poor young man in Midtown Manhattan because that is a place that is at once full of stuff and people and movement and, in certain states of mind, can feel kind of empty of meaning. To make Midtown sing the boy's song, I'll add details about souvenir stores with "I ♥ NY" shirts and mugs with the image of Donald Trump with his gunshot-wounded ear and his fist in the air and a "NEVER AGAIN" 9/11 snow globe. The trash cans on the street are overflowing and a well-dressed man stands looking at his phone while his fluffy white dog takes a shit on the sidewalk. These details pull the bigger world into the story. Maybe there's a news story on one of the big screens in Times Square about the war in Ukraine or about a blizzard coming. Maybe the war is something this young man is worried about. Maybe his dad is in the path of the blizzard. Maybe someone hands the boy a flyer for a pawn shop or an underground theater production of *Macbeth* or a pamphlet on Jesus. In any of those bigger-world introductions, there is an echo of the boy's feelings, plus the possibility of pushing him into a new place. What if he goes to the church listed in the pamphlet even though he hasn't been to church in ten years/is Jewish/is writing a dissertation on sex abuse in the church? What if he goes to the theater? What if he spends his twenty-seven dollars at the pawn shop on a bracelet he doesn't even think his dad will like? What if, when he walks out of the pawn shop, the blizzard looks like it's going to be bigger than expected?

Key

Begin in the interior and think about what your character is feeling. Now zoom up and out and look at the world around them. Is there weather that might echo or alter the interior landscape? Might this character be in a historical moment of importance, even if that event is not centered? Think about religion, money, current events of the day. None of these need to take over the story, unless you want them to. You are in control of all the volume knobs, so maybe you want the world to make a small chime or maybe you want a big, ringing gong. Get the world to play those notes for you, and let them resonate in the chest of the character, and in the world of the story.

DOORWAY #26

Write the Islands

Early Narrative Landscape

In a novel-writing class I taught, a group of brave graduate students entered a room in the chemistry building at Colorado State University in January with threads of ideas but nothing on the page. They walked out of the room for the last time in May with 150 pages each and a plan for how to continue. It was one of my favorite classes I've ever taught because we were all in the mystery together—no one knew what would emerge. It felt oddly appropriate that we were in the chemistry building, where our class was sometimes interrupted by the sound of some large, inscrutable science-y machine being wheeled down the hallway, and where formulas far beyond our literary comprehension were often scribbled on the whiteboard. We did not mix anything in beakers, but the creation of elements and narrative and characters felt so visceral in that room that it almost could have been bottled. We read many short novels to see how they worked, and the spine of our class was Matt Bell's wonderful book *Refuse to Be Done*. The book is full of ways to think about creating story, and ways to keep coming back. The idea we kept returning to over and over (and the one the writers from my class still talk about years later) was to "write the islands."

The islands, in this case, are the scenes and moments with

the most energy, excitement, heat, or magnetism. They are the bodies of land pushing up through the endless, depthless blue of the unknown ocean of this story. Bell notes that following your excitement will generate more excitement, while hammering through boredom usually creates more boredom. In a first draft (and, I'd argue, at all stages), giving yourself over to the most verdant, fruited, living parts of a story will lead you to the richest *complete* story, even if the islands appear separate from one another at first. Bridges can easily be built; boats can be sailed; islands grow bigger and connect.

By the end of the class, we each had an archipelago. We each had shores to land on, views of one island from another, rich soil full of weird fruits and creatures. There was so much life.

Key

Write the part that pulls you *today*. Write the scene that has heat for you right now. Your mantra is this: Do the next most-interesting thing. You do not, at this time, need connective tissue or even an understanding of how different parts of the story will come together. Write the islands. Trust that relationships between scenes and moments will emerge, in the same way the individual islands emerge. If your first draft is an archipelago of wild, life-filled islands, your second draft gets to be about finding and making connections, building bridges and floating boats, swimming over the fringy reef, which is as exploratory and fun. It never stops being the next most-interesting thing.

DOORWAY #27

Risk Sentimentality

The Heart Is a Messy Place

When I was writing my first novel, which draws on family stories from Romania, I spent hours every day in a world that felt sometimes impossibly dramatic and sad. Children died, villages were cleared out, people jumped in rivers to try and swim to safety. It was a lot. I wondered often if it was too much, too dark, and whether I as a young writer could handle this level of emotion. I also worried about putting horrors on the page for the easy narrative power they might provide. On one writing day when I was feeling unsure how to proceed, I took a break and read an interview in *Guernica* with Marlon James. James is the Booker Prize–winning author of five big, complicated novels including *Black Leopard, Red Wolf,* which is part fantasy, part history, and as ambitious as a book gets. In the interview he said something that stopped me in my tracks and completely changed how I approached my book:

> There's something to be read in the explicit scene. There's something to be read in being present in the uncomfortable moment. I'm not trying to bludgeon violence over someone's head, saying, "You need to experience it." I think if you're writing well you can get

> readers to read anything. The concern a lot of people have with explicit violence, explicit sex, explicit anything, is that it turns into a kind of pornography. And I am like, "So what?" Risk pornography. Risk it. Just like you have to risk sentimentality to get to sentiment. Risk pornography.
>
> It's better to have it down and pull back and pull out than to have this kind of failure of nerve and kid yourself that you're producing this sophisticated kind of art.

At the time it was the idea of opening the door to sentiment that struck me hardest and freed me most. I was never going to be able to write about war and loss without opening the door on the unwieldy, ferocious space of the heart. I was never going to be able to write losses well by writing them in a controlled or safe way. Safety was never the goal.

Key

Exposure is scary. It can feel safer to stay tucked in the land of intellect and argument and evidence than to head into the wilderness of feeling and experience. Safer, maybe, but never fully true. Risk sentimentality. Risk pornography. Risk excess. Put it all down. Find the broadest, deepest edges of the emotional landscape. Do not control for safety or tidiness. Later, you can pull back or distill, if that feels right. Better to have an overgrown forest than a bloodless rock.

DOORWAY #28

Against the Magnum Opus

Just This Day's Work

Writing a book is giant-sized in so many ways. Real resources must be spent—time, faith, sometimes money to make room for the time. You have to choose to believe in something you cannot see. You have to keep coming back and back and back. There's a lot of building of confidence in yourself and hyping the project in your own mind so that it feels worth your while. It's the Great American Surf Novel! It's the Great American Dog-Breeding Novel! It's the first memoir about a woman who ballet dances across Antarctica! No one has ever written a whole essay collection about ketchup before! Now presenting the complete poetics of snow!

It's beautiful, this part of the dance. The way you can make the lights come on with a little bit of pomp, a little bit of razzle-dazzle.

The trouble is that pretty soon the capital-I *Idea* can become heavy. The Great American anything is a container too big for one person to fill. The more pressure you put on this piece to be THE piece, your life's work, your opus, the harder it is to notice surprising new directions, to follow the energy, to be awake to what is truly alive on the page.

If I'm trying to write a masterpiece, I get worried every time I write a word that doesn't feel masterful, perfect. The Delete key gets worn with use and doubt.

Built into the fantasy of a Big Book is reception, praise, recognition. You're still on the first draft and already the lights of fame are in your eyes.

When I think of someone writing a masterwork, I picture a man with a gray beard working by candlelight in a turret with a view of a stormy ocean. At lunchtime, his servant brings him fish stew and thickly buttered bread. If a turret comes my way, I will totally pop my laptop open and see what happens, but at present I'm writing on my couch next to my sick child while watching *Despicable Me*. At some point I'll microwave some beans for us to eat. Luxury! I can't set out to write Great or Magnum on this couch. I can, however, do good work in this way, and since I don't seem to have a servant, a sea view, or a stone tower, this is the only way I have.

I want to be ambitious. I want to write novels I believe in, that matter to me, that maybe eventually matter to others too. For this to happen, I have to turn down the pressure. I have to do *this day's work*, this week's work. Exactly what each effort turns into will be revealed over time. Maybe there will be greatness somewhere in there. Maybe someone will blurb it and say, "This is the Great American Sick Kid on the Couch Novel." Who knows? But for now, I'm staying close to the ground because the ground is where things grow.

Key

When the pressure to make The One gets heavy, have a mantra ready. You can even put it on the wall. *The effort is the opus.* Or, *Everything together is the masterpiece.* Or, *No masterworks, only work.* Your work is the sum total of everything you have written and will write. That's the opus. Over all the days and weeks, you will hopefully write many things, and each of those pieces will matter in a different way. Maybe you get famous for a poem about toads that you wrote on a lark. What you are working on might feel like The One, and it is, for now. Happily, there will be new interests, new sparks.

DOORWAY #29

Write the Shit Out of Your Darlings

Indulgence as Doorway to Love

Somewhere mid-MFA I finally heard the old saw "kill your darlings." The idea is that we must be loyal to the piece rather than to ourselves, that if a scene or an image isn't working for the story, it has to go, even if it's the loveliest thing you've ever written. There is definitely truth in this, especially in late drafts.

Still, when someone said those words, I felt instantaneous terror. If we walk in the door of a piece not only with the fear that whatever we have to say is probably not that good, and we also walk in with a murder weapon designed to destroy anything we *do* like, well, that sounds like an ideal way to ensure that a person ceases to think of herself as a writer at all.

At an evening reading that I attended for the Writing Seminars at Bennington College, Claire Vaye Watkins read from an unpublished novel. It was the opening to a book about a woman living on a jackrabbit homestead in the Mojave Desert who has invited an old love to come care for her plants while she drives her daughter across the country. There were devastating passages about ecology and climate change, and people were also laughing hard at the bright, generous particularity of the character and voice. In the middle of the reading Claire paused and said, "Okay, I'm skipping a *big* section here about the plant instructions."

After the reading, Claire was swarmed with appreciators. I heard no fewer than four people tell her that they couldn't wait to read the novel to finally get the plant instructions. They were smiling but they were serious. Because it was clear from the reading that this passage would be filled with the character's weird, exact person-ness, that the plants were her proxies, that her instructions for their care would be her instructions for her own care. Also: because the author *wanted* to write them, so they would probably be interesting.

Let's imagine a pitch session at a big writers' conference. There are literary agents and aspiring authors and someone stands and asks, "Should I put several pages of plant-watering instructions in the opening chapter of my novel?" Nine out of ten agents probably roll their eyes.

I'm not telling you that every single version of plant instructions or their equivalent always stays in every single novel. Sometimes those details don't feel quite right. Sometimes six pages get trimmed into one paragraph. Sometimes, though, those six pages turn out to tell you what the whole damn book is about and you scrap the initial plot and go toward that curious little fire.

Key

Write the *shit* out of your darlings. Write the plant instructions like you freaking mean it. If your first draft is populated with your own curiosity and fury and laughter, with darling after darling after darling, that draft is a living thing. There is absolutely no way to have too much life in a piece of writing.

To write the shit out of your darlings requires you to be your own most important reader. To let the agent panel hang out in their conference room and talk about contract clauses. To let your parents or your sister or your teacher recede far into the background.

You will later organize, interrogate, trim, revise. Some darlings might be replanted in a smaller pot, some might go back into the greenhouse to be used in another story someday. All of that is as it should be. No one has to die here, least of all the dear, insane loves you yourself carry in your own dear, insane little heart. Grow those bulbs and stalks as big as you can. Let them take over the world.

DOORWAY #30

Do Your Worst

Abolish Shame by Writing Badly on Purpose

The beloved writer and teacher Alexander Chee talks about the connection between writer's block and shame. So often, we feel blocked because we are afraid that we are saying something stupid, that we will be outed as the frauds we all often feel like on the inside. We hesitate to put words on the page because they might out us as dummies, dorks, weirdos. Lines are written and erased and shame is reinforced. The blank page feels like proof that we were right, that we don't have anything worth writing, and when we return the next day, the weight of shame is heavier.

A way through: Write badly on purpose. When purple, horrendous prose is your point, shame can't touch you. Gross sentences and clichéd images are exactly what you *came* to do. Freeing and funny, these lines are a middle finger to feeling that you don't deserve to speak.

The nonfiction writer Eula Biss used this exercise in a class she taught during the pandemic, and she told me that it surprised all the students with its effectiveness and pleasure. They *loved* one another's bad writing. The terrible pages brought real joy to the group. And, very interestingly, little seeds of energy were born there. Seeds of permission to try something strange or still untested. Seeds of satire or humor. A feeling of powerful permission.

Key

Write badly for a whole page or two. Really, really lean in. Make yourself laugh. Make yourself queasy. Lay it on as thick as you can.

In Eula's class, part of the magic of this exercise came when the writers shared the work with one another. Do you have a writer friend to whom you might send your delicious worst?

And look at this—you've written a page or two. You've created feelings and characters out of words. Making something is making something. Tomorrow when you sit down to write, you'll do so with some wind in your sail.

DOORWAY #31

Dear Inner Asshole

The Devil's Email Address

You know how lots of people have a fake email address they use for promotional offers and other schlock? Instead of 20 percent off a sweater, this doorway will lead you to 20 percent fewer feelings of failure and at least a 30 percent increase in joy while writing.*

Go to your preferred email platform and create a new account. This email is the online address for your inner critic. Maybe you want to name him or her! Marsha or Roderick or JamesPAsshole@email.com. Selfdoubt2002 also works! Maybe you want to address your anxiety kindly or maybe you want to shout it out of the room (every day can be different!). Now you have contact information for a force responsible for messing with your writing life and they cannot block you! Let the spamming begin.

Dear Marsha,
I noticed you hanging out this morning in the shadows.
Go suck eggs!
Love,
Ramona

---

* These statements have not been evaluated by the FDA.

Hey Anxiety,

You keep me safe from kitchen fires and slipping on ice—thanks for that! I'm about to try to start a new novel and even though I appreciate you for so many things, this is one place where I kind of need you to go take a hot bath and leave me to make some mistakes. I promise I won't actually get hurt. I'll totally let you know when I'm going to chop wood so you can come help keep all my fingers attached.

Love you,

Ramona

Key

Name the force that slows or stops you from writing and make a place for it on the internet! Whenever you feel that dark shadow pop up, write a quick note to tell it to buzz off or say thanks but no thanks. I had an undergraduate student several years ago who started a conversation with her anxiety that itself turned into a long essay. Addressing this force directly can be not only cathartic but meaningful. It's part of you.

Part 2

DOORWAY #32

Scissors and Glue

Rearrange, Resee

We write in whatever order the ideas occur to us, or in the logic of our original vision. How it comes is how it comes. But how it comes is not how it necessarily has to or wants to stay. I say constantly to my students that every part is a moving part. This includes choices about point of view and setting and time period and voice and every other craft-level decision we writers make. It also includes the structure of each scene or line and the piece as a whole. How it is built is part of what it *is* and *does.*

I am a cut-and-paste superfan. Reordering can completely change the way a story feels. When a document is open on the screen, it's essentially a very long scroll, and while sentence-level changes or plopping a paragraph from page 1 to page 3 is easy, bigger rearrangements get difficult to track. This is when it's time to print the whole thing out and get physical.

Key

Print what you have and gather scissors and, if you want, a glue stick and some blank paper. Depending on what you have, you'll cut the piece into different-sized sections. For a short story, I usually cut at the scene level. If it's a poem, you can cut at the line level. Rearrange. You can glue your reordered version down on the blank paper and then reprint, rearrange, and glue again to see another possibility. If you are working on a bigger scale (rather than line by line), you might not need the glue but could simply take photos of different arrangements.

Step two is to read these versions and take note of what they do and how they feel. Feel free to repeat the process now that you have a sense of what changes when you make these kinds of moves. Once you have a new order you're into (for now! It can change again and again!), go back to your document, Save As so you don't lose any history, and make the shifts there. This is now your working draft.

DOORWAY #33

Get Out of Your Known World

Write What You *Want* to Know

The old "write what you know" advice is one way to reach toward a subject that might generate energy and words on the page. Your lived experience can, indeed, be a depthless and rich well.

"Write what you know" does not mean write *only* what you know.

You also get to write your curiosities, your unanswerable questions, your obsessions. Write about desert plants, 1980s aerobics instructors, a high-end restaurant kitchen, elephant research, cabinetry, oil spills, Arctic icebreakers, a chair that's been passed through six generations, the third moon landing, a woman caught in an essential oil multilevel marketing scheme. You can say a lot of things about the world but not that it's boring. I keep a list of curiosities. Did you know that there are professional mourners in some parts of the world? That there is a person who will go to work tonight at your local zoo to give all the animals their evening meal and turn off their lights like in the picture book my kids loved? There is a creature in the Bornean rain forest called the slow loris, which is a tiny primate with big eyes, but also one of the only venomous mammals.

In the end, if I choose to write toward an external curiosity, something I want to know, I'll probably put a lot of my own lived experience in there too. Luckily there is no prohibition on mixing, even if you write nonfiction. You won't claim to be that nighttime zookeeper, but you might write a braided essay about caregiving that includes that person and what you learn about their job. Or, if you are a fiction writer, you get to imagine your way into the space where orangutans curl up in moppy heaps and the hippo likes to have her butt scratched before going to bed.

A small note: There is reason to worry about writing beyond our own experience when it comes to significant difference. A straight, cisgender writer like me is so obviously not the one to take on a first-person story about a transgender man. My rule is that I don't stake a claim to something that doesn't belong to me. I try to be very honest and ask myself if there is potential to cause harm.

Key

Start a list of curiosities. These can be anything at all! What do airline pilots talk about on a long flight? What was up with the hole in the ozone layer discovered in the eighties? Super-niche dog breeds! Russian ballet! People who surf in shark-infested waters! Intimacy coordinators on film sets!

Take pleasure in falling down some rabbit holes.

Let these curiosities and discoveries inhabit your work, whether they are at the center or a small thread.

One of the joys of being a writer is that you get to make it your business—your *job*—to find out about the world.

Maybe the shark-infested waters become the backdrop for a love story between two surfers. Maybe the hole in the ozone layer is a tiny detail in a story about a group of friends. Maybe the main character quits her job in sales to breed Italian truffle-hunting dogs.

DOORWAY #34

Fairy Tale-ify

Using "Once upon a Time" to Find the Frame

Former Pixar story artist Emma Coats once tweeted one of the studio's framing devices. It's useful exactly because it's highly simplified, designed to give me a sense of what I do and do not know about the big-picture scaffolding of my current story. This structure won't truly fit rangier work, and you shouldn't feel that you must force it to. Instead of being a structure you must conform to, this structure feels to me like a kind of magnifying glass to peek through. It tells me as much about how I want to break with convention as it does about how much I want to follow it. It goes like this:

Once upon a time . . .
And every day . . .
Until one day . . .
And because of this . . .
And because of this . . .
Until finally . . .
And ever since that day . . .

You can see how neatly every conventional film fits into this frame. And yet it gives you a tiny little map for the bigger idea, and a tiny map that you can glance at in one second can be a great gift.

Key

Try to plug your piece (or what you know of it) into this frame. Maybe it becomes the navigational tool in the way it was intended—hooray if so! Maybe it becomes a kind of anti-map—a way of seeing how you don't want to follow conventional narrative—hooray if so!

This is a tool to revisit as your sense of the object changes.

DOORWAY #35

A Portrait in Objects

Defining Characters by the Things They Love and Carry

Every time I think I should cycle Tim O'Brien's seminal *The Things They Carried* off my syllabus, the next group of students is as moved and enamored as every previous class. If you haven't read it, or haven't read it in a while, it's a collection of linked short stories about a group of young American men fighting in the Vietnam War, but instead of starting with their histories, their mission, their fear, the first piece introduces them by way of the things they are each carrying with them.

The story begins:

> First Lieutenant Jimmy Cross carried letters from a girl named Martha, a junior at Mount Sebastian College in New Jersey. They were not love letters, but Lieutenant Cross was hoping, so he kept them folded in plastic at the bottom of his rucksack. In the late afternoon, after a day's march, he would dig his foxhole, wash his hands under a canteen, unwrap the letters, hold them with the tips of his fingers, and spend the last hour of light pretending.

Later, we get this passage:

> On ambush, or other night missions, they carried peculiar little odds and ends. Kiowa always took along his New Testament and a pair of moccasins for silence. Dave Jensen carried night-sight vitamins high in carotene. Lee Strunk carried his slingshot; ammo, he claimed, would never be a problem. Rat Kiley carried brandy and M&M's candy. Until he was shot, Ted Lavender carried the starlight scope, which weighed 6.3 pounds with its aluminum carrying case. Henry Dobbins carried his girlfriend's pantyhose wrapped around his neck as a comforter. They all carried ghosts.

The things we keep, hold, surround ourselves with, lose, love, say so much about who we are and where we are. They are our fears and our history and our hope. They have weight.

Key

Write a portrait of a character in objects. What does she carry in her bag? What is on her nightstand, in the back of her underwear drawer? What is one thing she should get rid of but cannot? What is something she lost and still misses? What does she carry that is nonphysical (like the platoon's ghosts)? What thing or things would she be embarrassed by if someone discovered them? What does she display as a way to prove herself?

DOORWAY #36

Time Travel

Take a Trip to the Distant Past, the Far Future, or Five Minutes from Now

Sometimes it feels like writing is a form of muck-slog, my feet sucked into the soft mud, and there are cattails and vines blocking my view. I am in it. It's easy to become a bog mummy. But then I remind myself that I am a writer so I don't need an as-yet-uninvented technology to move through time or space. I can fly to any point in the entire history of the world, to any place on earth or beyond, or to futures unknown!

Reminding myself of this helps me to realize that what I'm writing is a single point in a vast sky. That there are secrets and surprises to be discovered, relationships and constellations to be drawn by doing some *Magic School Bus*–style journeying.

Key

Head to the future! What is this character doing in six months, in five years, on their deathbed? What does the story's landscape look like in a century? What beautiful or terrible event might happen here next fall? What blossoms or fruit are quietly waiting for the spring thaw? Someday, will this woman hold her twin grandchildren on this same porch?

Now, the past! We're used to thinking about backstory and key moments in the past that explain the present (for example, a moment from childhood when the character's dad hit him, tucked between scenes of his current alcoholism and dangerous temper), but I like the practice of time traveling to moments that might not necessarily seem immediately relevant, because that's where the unexpected treasure is. What happened in this spot a thousand years ago? What was that alcoholic character's favorite class in high school? What was the first song he really loved? Was there an old house that stood here before the current apartment building was put up? Who planted those deep-purple tulips? Is there anything weird buried in the yard? Hidden in the walls?

Dig until the terrain changes. Fly until you've got a new view.

DOORWAY #37

Hit the Road

Journey Across Land and Sea

Time travel is only one way of finding unknown or hidden details and possibilities. If I'm in that murky bog, it's time to hop in the car or charter a flight to anywhere else. I think of the watershed where my piece takes place and go look at the headwaters of the river and the delta where it eventually empties. I want to know if there are eggs in the nest in the pine tree in the front yard outside the little girl's window. Where is the cemetery where the grandparents are buried? Let's go look at the crumbling old high school. Is there a container ship leaving port, bound for the other side of the world, carrying an item that will later matter to this piece? Or maybe we can trace the blue sweater the mother wears back to the factory where it was sewn.

As with the time travel, I'm not committed to including any of these excursions in the story or essay itself. Very often something will stick, but even if it doesn't, I have almost always come to a richer or fresher understanding of the world of the story. I've opened myself up beyond the expected. My view is bigger and so is my reach.

Key

If your story takes place in a mountain town, maybe you'd like to know what is happening eighty miles away, by the sea. What weather is brewing there that will soon reach your characters? Is there someone on the lonely highway, headed right this way? What's happening under the surface of the earth? What's happening inside a character's body?

Go exploring. You can do this in sentences or paragraphs or in a list. Revisit this and add to it. The wider your landscape, the more you have to draw from when you're feeling small.

DOORWAY #38

In the Beginning

Every Story Is an Origin Story

My students like to talk about the "inciting incident." The fire that changed a neighborhood and a girl's life, the moment when the main character's crush pulled someone else into a kiss, the day the mother brought a wild possum into the house. This is an event after which nothing is the same. The inciting incident is a perfectly valid frame, but for some reason it makes me feel a little . . . sad. The language is that of a device, a manipulation. It makes me feel like I'm writing in a corporate boardroom and making choices designed to extract desired reactions from predetermined readers.

I prefer to ask myself a question like this: What is being born here, now? In what way is this moment the origin of something living, never before seen? In the beginning there was . . .

In the beginning there was a wild possum in my kitchen.

In the beginning my mother wrapped the possum in my old baby blanket.

In the beginning the possum made my mother less sad than she had been in two years.

Not only does this create electricity from the sense that the lives of these characters are about to begin again, but my writer brain starts buzzing with possibilities: Why has Mom been so sad for two years? What does it feel like to watch a woman find solace in an animal when she does not seem to find solace in her human child? What will this wild animal do to the family, both physically and emotionally? There is so much I'm curious about!

I realize that this framing is a subtle difference, and if the "inciting incident" language works for you, please proceed with it!

For me, the more I write in a space of wonder, the more interesting my work is (and the happier I am while making it). An origin story is a place of wonder. How did we get this world? How did we find ourselves here, in this wild land?

The origin story gives me permission to imagine that what I'm writing is the beginning of something big, because even a small event can feel monstrous or enormous to the person it happens to. Isn't that what it is to be a person? In each of us is a landscape of feeling and experience so vast it could take up the entire universe. If I am taking my work seriously, that landscape of experience does take up the entire universe, because the story belongs to that character. These scenes are, in a real way, the beginning of the world.

Key

Start with and repeat the phrase "In the beginning . . ."

You do not need to keep this language in later drafts (though you certainly can).

Even after you have moved past the moments of beginning-ness, keep asking yourself how this piece is an origin story. What is born here? In what way will the world never be the same? Let the heat of that significance be a kind of power source.

DOORWAY #39

The Era Of

Define Your Own Epoch

This is a cousin of the origin story, but instead of finding the frame, it looks for details that populate this space.

When our kids were in preschool, a mom friend said, "This is the era of only eating quesadillas and everyone fighting to push the elevator button." Small details are the substance of life in a certain time, an individual epoch in one's life. The details *are* the life. And then things change and you realize you haven't made a quesadilla in two years.

Right now, in my house, it's the era of saying to my thirteen-year-old boy, "Can you take your headphones off so we can have this conversation?" It's the era of my girl standing on her hands as much as she stands on her feet. It's the era of packing her a lunch and then unpacking the same lunch, largely untouched, seven hours later.

Key

Look for patterns and habits in the lives of your characters. What is it about their *now* that shapes this time? Is it the era of saying hello to the old woman on the bus who wears a fur coat and plastic shower caps rubber-banded over her boots? Is it the era of the woman's boss asking again if she has children? Is it the era of the breast pump in the office bathroom?

To pay attention to details-as-defining-moment is to honor the way a distinct time has its own texture and reality. It reminds us that things were not always this way and will change and change and change, making the present, this era, precious and precise, fleeting.

DOORWAY #40

What We're Worried About

Finding Humanity (and Your Character) in Anonymous Email Help Lists from the Early 2000s

Before social media and even before Google reviews or Yelp, I lived in Berkeley, California, and subscribed to the Berkeley Parents Network email list. I was eighteen years old, not a parent, not even in the realm of potential parenthood, but this was the place where you could find out where to get shoes for high arches, who knew a good plumber, and whether that sound in the attic was a rat. I think I first looked at the list to see if anyone had advice about where to get my curly hair cut, which was an event that had previously always left me in tears.

The email went out weekly, each one containing a series of new questions and a series of answers to previous questions. What I did not see coming was the depth of humanity I would find in those emails. They revealed to me everything that my neighbors were afraid of, what they were suffering with, and what they desired. The range was gorgeous: Does anyone want the boulder we'll dig out when we renovate our yard? Is it okay to leave my fifteen-year-old home alone for the night? Is there something wrong with a kid who is average? Does everyone need to excel?

Not only were the questions tender and honest; so too were the responses. Many of the emails are archived and you can read both questions and answers, which give tremendous insight into the inner lives of other people.

Here's the list of subject lines from the questions in one email from my early days as a subscriber:

11 yo pooping in shower (ugh)
Moving
Nanny-share: What do you pay?
Osteopenia
Postmenopausal blood levels without other symptoms
Potty Training 4 yo boy. I'm worried; he's not.
Terminally absent-minded husband
Toilet finish looking gray inside
Tonsillectomy Recovery for an Adult
Too expensive to visit in-laws
Traffic ticket not online or by phone
Transitional Swaddle
Used clothes - is donation or consignment better?
Voiceover work for kids
Working with dreams

Look at us human animals with so much we don't know, so many needs, so much we can't do alone. And it's all happening at once! The terminally absent-minded husband is contiguous with the toilet looking gray and the child pooping in the shower and the unworn clothes and the confusing dreams. Our inner lives are vast and they are mundane. They are unique and they are universal. We are containers of worry and hope. What is writing for, if not a path through that realm?

Key

Make a list of all the things a character is worried about. Explore the big and deep and explore the everyday. What would she ask about if she thought the response would be generous? What is she too afraid to say out loud?

Make the same list for a different character. The mother or the partner or the child, say.

Take on the unspoken, the unseen. Is Mom worried about her preteen daughter's difficulty choosing what to wear in the morning while the daughter is worried about getting food in her teeth at lunch and being made fun of? In that white space of what is not spoken, you've found a line of tension.

BONUS KEY

Look through the archives of this list (berkeleyparents network.org) or another space like it and find questions or details that enliven your imagination or fill out worlds beyond your own.

DOORWAY #41

The Haunting

Every Story Is a Ghost Story

At a big gathering, a woman who claimed to be a psychic told my friend Stuart that he was surrounded by dead people. He laughed and said, "I mean, definitely." Isn't everybody, though? We are all alive at this precise moment on a planet once inhabited by billions of people and animals and trees no longer here in body. The dead far outnumber the living.

I have written some stories with actual ghosts in them, and I love a good ghost story. The way it feels to pull away the veil between what is and what was and to build anew the rules for this crossing.

But there does not need to be a misty undead presence for a story or essay or poem to be haunted. A question can haunt a piece or a character. A memory can be a kind of ghost. The presence of things unseen has a major effect on the present and on living people and events.

Key

Go on a ghost hunt! Get your *Ghostbusters*-style Psychokinetic Energy Meter and scan your current piece or idea for invisible presences. Who is here, even if they are not here? What hangs over the scene? What mysterious weight is the character holding?

Once you know what's haunting this world, your next job is to press those forces onto the page, even in small ways. Let the aura of a concern—something in the mind or heart—change what someone *does*. Let the ghosts, whether figurative or literal, start to materialize.

DOORWAY #42

Setting as Window

Texture and Seeing in the Cereal Boxes, the Dry Grass, the Empty Pool

Imagine a space: The window curtains are heavy velvet, blocking out all light. There are six fragile porcelain teacups on the bedside table, each of them stained. It's a canopy bed, dark wood, intricately carved, but it's also a twin-size, much less wide than it is tall.

The bookcase contains an entire shelf of financial self-help. Look up: This is not a fancy room with molding and beautiful wood floors. It's got cheap tan carpet and orange-peel texture on the walls. The ceiling is popcorn, probably full of asbestos.

I don't know who lives here, but I'm curious. Someone who has lost almost everything? Someone who has climbed this far but can't get to the next rung? A very old person? A former frat boy who inherited his grandmother's furniture?

Our spaces reflect both our circumstances and our inner selves. They reveal striving and failure. They reveal history and inheritance, late-night purchases, nostalgia.

Key

Go for a walk around the houses, apartments, office cubicles, and front yards of your characters. Rummage through their cars. How would they describe the spaces? What are they proud of? Embarrassed by? What do they hide when someone is coming over for dinner? Are there things someone else in their life feels weird about? Jealous of? What's in that box on the front stoop? What's in the unmarked envelope on the kitchen table?

Not all the details need to end up in the draft, but seeing a person's home and the other spaces they inhabit will always give you information and texture about the life or lives that take place within those walls.

DOORWAY #43

Be a Good Host for Your Art

If Your Project Tries to Run Away, You Won't Get It to Come Home by Yelling

When my friend Matt's daughter Evie was in kindergarten, she got very angry about something now lost to history and she announced that she was running away from home. She went upstairs to her room and put on a fancy dress and her fake pearls and her dress-up shoes and packed a bag with more jewelry, more fancy dresses, and a stuffed animal. She said her goodbyes and walked out the back door. Matt watched her cross the yard and enter the playhouse and shut the door behind her.

A sweet dad, he gave her a little while—fifteen minutes, maybe twenty—to live this new independent life. When he went out, he knocked on the door. She opened it a crack and he asked if he could come over to her house for a few minutes. She agreed. Inside he saw that she had hung her dresses on the backs of the small chairs and laid her necklaces out on the play kitchen counter.

"What a nice house you have," he said. "You really know how to make things homey."

"Thank you."

"I want you to know that you can still come visit us in the other house anytime. We'll keep your room for you. If it's cold out here, you could always sleep in there."

They spent another few minutes chatting and then Evie suggested that she might like to visit her dad and the rest of the family in their house that night.

They walked back together.

In another story, the dad yells at his daughter not to even think about running away. In another story he rolls his eyes at her outfit and tells her she won't last five minutes, then told-you-sos when she comes back inside. In another story he carries her upstairs. Even if all of these possibilities end with the girl asleep in her own bed that night, in only one does the relationship between adult and child grow stronger.

This is a very sweet story about parenting and giving kids dignity and respect (and a story about patience! so much patience!), and it's also a story about how to offer those same things to your writing.

I was working on a new draft when I heard this story, and I had a flash of recognition: I had been carrying my writing up the stairs against its will while it yelled in my ear. I had been forcing it. I had not been kind when it got tangled. If I wanted the relationship between me and my piece to be stronger, I was going to have to befriend the tangle. I was going to have to appreciate its string of fake pearls and impractical shoes and weird little heart.

Key

Look at your piece like a kid who wants your love. Like a fresh being, unsure how to live out loud, trying its best. You can banish it, yell at it, scold it, talk shit about it to your friends, but is any of that really going to make your relationship to the work stronger? Even if novels don't have feelings (my fingers resist typing that—it feels not completely true), *you* are part of the novel and you definitely have a real, living relationship with the world and the characters you are creating. When a story has tried to run from you, try visiting it in its hideout. Bring tea and cookies. See and praise its heart. Promise a warm bed as soon as it's ready to come home.

DOORWAY #44

The Language of Work

Texture and Seeing in the Hammer, the Blackboard, the Sail

We recently had to replace our furnace and I spent a few weeks talking with HVAC people. This lexicon is full of words like "pressure," "dual-stage valve," "efficiency," and "therms." I like these words even though I don't really know what they mean or how this big underground system keeps my house warm. One day, a nice guy said to me, "With the higher-end blower, you'll have less feathering of air pressure," which I did not understand but thought was quite lovely.

I liked looking at my whole house, my whole life, through the lens of the heating, ventilation, and air-conditioning system for a while. I liked the language, but it was also about a way of paying attention to the world. If I'm an HVAC technician, I see the inner workings of a house as much as the outside.

This is not an argument for believability, like throwing a tool belt on a character as a cue. This is about a way of seeing and being in the world. Let's say the mom in our story works in HVAC and her whole day is spent going down into the hidden underworlds of people's homes—ducts, condensers, inflow and output, feathered air pressure. How else might this affect the way she lives? Does she think about tubing, about air pressure, when she looks at her new baby? Does she see the hidden machinery in her boyfriend's life? Is she happier in the dank crawl spaces of the world than she is in the light?

Everyone's language is built of different parts. Regional words, sounds, dialects; family habits, inside jokes, vocabulary; then there's the way Grandma always talked about her rock-hounding, the way Dad kept his industrial sewing machine organized, the way Mom's legal briefs swam through her head when she was trying to read to the kids at night.

Key

Crack open the language of work by writing the jobs or occupations (even if the work isn't paid, it still matters) your characters have. Write the words and associations you have with the work. Now it's time for an internet rabbit hole! I like Reddit for nerding out on insider knowledge I don't understand. You can always look to trade magazines, fan sites, or social media affinity groups. Find schools or classes where this job or skill is taught and read their class descriptions and book lists. If you really get into it, you could find a local meetup group and go ask questions.

You don't have to weigh down your pieces with thousands of details of on-the-job terminology. A little bit stands in for a lot more. That being said, if you get really into a subculture and it keeps feeding new energy into the writing, then you can keep burrowing in that hole until you pop out somewhere new.

DOORWAY #45

The Language of Pleasure

Feeling and Seeing Through Sex, Food, and Beauty

In every piece of writing, there is a relationship with pleasure, even if it's quiet or filtered through pain. I want to draw a broad line around the idea of pleasure.

Sex is certainly there, and the entire universe of physical and emotional pleasure surrounding the act itself. Sex can be profound or mundane. It can be scary or it can be beautiful. It is always a singular moment even if it's also part of a routine or a pattern.

Food is a core source of pleasure in a thousand different ways. Think of how it would feel if a food from your childhood appeared before you exactly as it used to be. Think of sitting down to a table so laden with beautiful dishes that you could eat until it hurt. Think of someone handing you a slice of freshly baked bread, still warm from the oven and thick with butter. Think of picking sun-warm blackberries, your wrists scratched and your hands red with juice.

Sometimes beauty in writing works as a backdrop. Maybe there's a lovely mountain range the angry couple hikes while they fight. Maybe the sunset makes an appearance or a woman is compared to a famous painting. What I want to think about here is what happens when the beauty—whether from nature, art, or an act of service—moves from being a passive backdrop to an active pleasure. Once this happens, the chemistry of the character, image, or moment changes because beauty has been internalized. Pleasure creates movement, and movement changes what happens next.

Key

Write for twenty minutes about a character's relationship with pleasure. What does this person delight in? What would they drive two hours out of their way to eat? Which desires pull them, even if there's a shadow side? Do they go out of their way to fulfill the desires of others, even if they themselves take no pleasure there? What would they ask for if they knew the request would be met without judgment? List the things they secretly love and the things they adore out loud.

Time for another internet rabbit hole! Maybe your character is obsessed with frog-shaped stuffed animals—go find the world of others who also think and breathe this exact joy, and use the language of the different qualities of frog stuffie, the characters in that world. Look up discussions of the world's best key lime pie and gather notes about how the consistency and flavor are evaluated and appreciated.

Take one or more of those pleasures and move them into action. Maybe the character really does drive two hours out of her way to eat her late mom's favorite tamales. Let something happen as a result of this: She calls her grandmother for the first time since . . . ; she finds a stray cat outside the restaurant and adopts it; she meets someone who knew her mom; she decides to open her own tamale stand. Or maybe she drives all that way and the tamales taste like tamales to her, are not transcendent, do not offer magical access to her mom, and the revelation is that the woman has to find her own source of desire and meaning.

DOORWAY #46

POV Switch

Finding the Story in Perspective

My first novel was about a group of Jewish villagers in Romania in 1939, when the country was on the cusp of war. I wrote the novel in a collective "we" voice because that was what felt true to me. The story did move to individual people, but for many drafts the novel as a whole was equally held by the group. I knew that this was a hard choice, a big choice, especially since I was writing a novel for the very first time. There was a lot of energy, for me, in that plural perspective. Many drafts later and after much rejection, I allowed myself to open to the idea that for this novel to make that necessary transfer from my pages to a reader's head and heart, it needed a main character. We needed a center, a home.

For one week I went through the manuscript and changed "we" to "she" so that one woman was at the center. I also kept many passages with the chorus since I had always understood this to be collective story and did not want to lose that. I knew within a few pages that this combination was a much sturdier and fuller expression of the story. The collective was completely present, unquestionably important, and even more poignant within the ache of individual loneliness and struggle. It almost felt as if that both-ness of the "we" and the "she" had been there all along. As if there were no other way it ever could have happened.

Because experience is so personal, shifting perspective can completely change the way a scene or story or moment feels. In college my professor assigned an exercise where we wrote the Garden of Eden story from the perspective of anything other than Adam or Eve—the snake, the apple, the tree. It's a different story when it belongs to the tree that was made to grow the forbidden fruit.

Key

Switch the point of view. In this case, point of view refers to the narrator—first person (I), second person (you), third person (he/she/they). See what it feels like to write the moment in the first person instead of the third. See what it feels like to have an omniscient point of view that can see and know what every single character is thinking and feeling.

Or switch perspective. If you started through the daughter's eyes, rewrite the scene from the mother's view. Write a moment neither of them knows about from the father's telling. What does the dog know?

Since this is exploratory, try something even less familiar and ask the garbage collector in the neighborhood what she's seen in the trash. See what the mail carrier knows about everyone from the letters he delivers. Follow the dog walker around. The little girl's teacher.

Even a paragraph is enough to bring new light or air into the situation.

DOORWAY #47

The Detail Journal

Pay Attention to the Plentiful Wonder Around You

One spring we had so much rain in Colorado that little pools of water appeared in the wells of the sprinkler heads. Water in the West is always a good thing, and everything felt green and abundant. One day I was in the yard and I noticed something moving in one of these micro-ponds. A frog! A tiny thing, living in a tiny, temporary pool of water. Where had this frog come from? I wondered. There was no way this animal had hopped here. I realized there must have been eggs underground, dormant and waiting for a wet season. The rain would stop, though, and then what? I didn't want this miraculous little hopper to dry out. My daughter suggested that we take a photo of the frog and send it to her friend Micah, then six years old, who fancied himself an expert herpetologist. Micah identified the species and suggested we transport the animal to a bigger pond in a nearby park. I caught the frog in a yogurt container, and we drove it to its new home less than a mile away. My daughter and I walked in the mud to the edge of the water and let our new friend go, wishing it all the very best.

There was so much meaning and possibility in this moment: water in a dry place, life emerging seemingly from nowhere, impending death, an expert who also happened to be in kindergarten, salvation in the form of a yogurt container and a city park, the understanding that even in the bigger pond, spring would end, summer would be hot, and the frog would not always be here. This would have disappeared into my memory or been forgotten if not for a key tool: the detail journal.

If the problem is lack of material or matter, I borrow some. The world creates and serves up terrible, gorgeous, funny, and strange facts and details all the time. Paying attention is a potent antidote to being stuck. Paying attention isn't enough though, at least for me, because I forget things, so I have to write them down. This journal is where my little frog friend lives.

The more I put myself in the business of noticing, the more the world around me provides matter that keeps my stories alive. The writer Pam Houston calls these details served up by the world "glimmers." Some other recent journal entries: the giant semitruck car carrier I saw broken down on the side of I-70 in western Colorado, only instead of Buicks, it was loaded with two levels of hearses; the dad I saw in Mexico who dug a hole big enough to stand in, stood in the hole for a good hour, and then left the beach; the Airbnb host who met us at the door of our rented house and described the other houses on his property this way: "We've got the male hut, which is the shape of the male anatomy, and we've got the female hut, which is the shape of a womb. As for beds, there's five twins in the uterus, plus a queen in the ball sack." When I'm stuck, I go looking through this journal. A detail is a doorway. Great details can absolutely make a story for a reader, but they can also make a story *possible* for a writer. A detail is a lantern that makes enough light to see by.

Key

Write down every interesting thing you see for a week. It doesn't always have to be dramatic. Maybe it's the wilting peonies in front of the dentist's office. Maybe it's the smell of the pan you left on the stove too long. Put yourself in the business of paying attention. The more you notice, the more you notice. And the longer the list is, the more it becomes a source. Consider keeping a list in two places: one on paper and one in your phone. When you're stuck in your writing, go to the detail journal and see where that lantern light might lead you.

DOORWAY #48

Read!

Fall into Another Mind's Genius

Like walking, this one seems too simple, but it's one of the most reliable doorways I know.

I read for technique and craft, to be sure. I read to learn how this author uses second person and how that author creates dramatic tension in an otherwise quiet scene. Describing it this way makes it sound so much more logical than it feels, though. So much of what I'm doing when I read is about giving myself over to someone else's care and creation. Another human being spent hundreds or thousands of hours in this world, following their own instincts, desires, worries. They wanted it to come through for me, this unknown body on the other side. They wanted the story to belong to me too.

When I'm stuck, reading is especially about finding permission and energy. Right now I'm reading Karen Russell's newest novel, *The Antidote*. It's about a witch who can take in other people's memories, but it's also about the Dust Bowl and girls' high school basketball and teen mothers and growing up poor. The permission I'm taking is about the way Russell opens her arms to make space for ideas that another writer would never put together. In every thread of the novel, I can feel the author's fullhearted curiosity and interest. Her energy becomes my energy, even if I'm not directly trying to use a technique she employs.

My students are often afraid that they'll copy someone else or that they'll be unable to tell the difference between inspiration and their own voice. In almost every case, we become clearer about our own perspective the longer we keep writing. Even if we start in one place, mimicking a text, we'll move in the direction of our own perspective.

Key

For this doorway, pick a book that is not direct research for your writing project. Instead, choose something where you can let yourself be carried, rather than having to drive the inquiry. Thirty minutes of reading time takes you far from your day-to-day. Read one short story, one essay, or a chapter of a novel. Two or three poems can shift your perspective.

Literature is an ocean you can swim in. Float on your back and let it hold you up.

DOORWAY #49

Eff It, I'm Just Going To . . .

What Would You Do If No One Were Watching?

Years ago, at a makeshift writing residency organized by a few friends, I was suffering through a hard draft of my second novel, *Sons and Daughters of Ease and Plenty*, and trying to figure out how to proceed. I was pregnant and afraid that if I didn't finish the book before the baby was born, I would never finish it and then I would never write anything ever again. I went out of my room to find someone to complain to and came upon Marie-Helene Bertino. I wanted her to tell me that it was okay to give the heck up, but instead she said, "Maybe you should do the thing that seems like the most fun." This hit me like a tropical rainstorm, warm and surprising and right. I kept this mantra close to me for the duration of that novel, and it guided me in energetic and interesting directions again and again.

Writing is such very hard work and we all want to be taken seriously and it's easy to forget that pleasure and joy are allowed and welcome, even when the writing itself is full of difficult material. We want and need to write toward the hardest loss, toward vast pain. What would be the most fun? And also, what would be the most meaningful? The scariest?

Fun isn't always Ferris wheels and funnel cake. That's why this is the "Eff It, I'm Just Going To . . ." doorway. This is where you throw your arms up and let go of expectation and fear and write toward the real thing. Write it for yourself. This is like the "dance as if no one is watching" draft, but with more swearing. Eff it, I'm just going to tell the truth about what my relationship with my father is like. Eff it, I'm just going to make the sister a mermaid. Eff it, I'm going to write this novel in first person plural. Eff it, I'm going to write this story in the voice of a cactus.

Sometimes, as with any attempt, this doesn't come out quite right. The cactus keeps morphing into an old man, or the old man keeps morphing into a cactus. I encourage you to keep listening and keep trusting. It's okay if it gets weirder or if it gets less weird.

Maybe I set a novel in Italy because that would make it possible for me to *have* to go to Italy and write the trip off on my taxes. No one can stop me from doing that. I can't always *afford* to do this, but it's the same permission slip as choosing to make a character a pastry chef and then going on a cake tour of my city, tasting everything.

When I was a kid, my best friend and I did a lot of scheming. We schemed for more time together, for treats, for new shoes, for excursions to the zoo or the movies. We were in cahoots and we were quite convincing. When we were ten, we were particularly enamored of the Dairy Queen Peanut Buster Parfait, and once we managed to get my mom to drive us across town for one even though it was late and she was already in her pajamas. I felt very, very powerful and also very happy in that moment. The "Eff It" doorway is about approaching your work in a similar way.

Key

It's you in cahoots with your writing. Scheme. Write in such a way that it feels like a secret plan. Write what feels like the most fun. Write the thing you have always felt forbidden from.

You and your pages are trying to convince someone to drive you to a fast-food restaurant for a cold, ridiculous treat at 9 p.m. on a Thursday, and the two of you are impossible to resist. No one can resist you.

DOORWAY #50

Ask What a Character Wants to Tell You

On Listening

In one of my favorite experiences of my life, I was matched as a mentor with a luminescent writer named Jamie Figueroa in the MFA program at the Institute of American Indian Arts. I was a white faculty member in a Native-serving institution, and I was nervous for many good reasons. Except that Jamie was not a stranger, even though we hadn't ever met. Oh, it's *you*, I thought. I was technically her teacher, but I have learned at least as much from her as she ever did from me.

Jamie approaches the characters in her pages as more than fictional constructions. It's not that they're real living people. Jamie knows she is in the story as a creator who has the job of shaping and pressing characters into being. There is real life in fictional characters, even still. Memory, lived experience, shared experience, the great force of imagination and empathy and care beyond our own skin. There is real feeling, real energy, and certainly real meaning in made-up people. Once a relationship is established between a living body and a person on the page, the page person begins a kind of life in the real world.

Having acknowledged that characters are present and embodied, Jamie asks them questions. What do they want her to know? What are they afraid for her to know? This is partly a way of asking herself what *she* knows (maker that she is), but it's also a way to appreciate that not all knowledge is conscious, that not all wisdom is earned via a linear course of study.

Not only is a piece of writing a collaboration between writer and reader, it is a collaboration between writer and everything that is. God, if you want, or the universe, or the planet, or the forever-chain of ancestors, or simply all the hearts beating across all the lands, right now.

Key

Write a letter to you, from a character. Let them speak to you directly and tell you what they know, what they want, what they're afraid of.

Write a letter from one character to another. See if things are revealed in this relationship that haven't been revealed before.

Ask your character questions and write their answers down. Ask things outside the immediate scope of the story. Find out about their hygiene habits, their recurring dreams, the nicknames their mom still calls them by. What kind of cereal do you like? What time each day do you start drinking? Try conducting the interview as yourself, the writer, or as another person in the story.

If you want to push this to a whole new level, have someone (or a group of people—your writing group?) interview you as one of your characters. They'll ask you things you might not think of.

DOORWAY #51

The Clock

Every Story Lives in a Time Frame

Every story has a clock. It could be dramatic, as in the time it takes to get to the hospital from the cabin where a man has chopped off his pinky. It could be the time it takes to dig out the archaeological remains of a city or the nine innings of a baseball game or the length of one night, the length of a war or the length of a character's sobriety. Some stories have very quiet clocks, and some are propelled in a large way by that ticking. There are stories that take place in one day or one week. Stories where the bomb is going to explode in thirty-six minutes unless our heroes dismantle it.

Two men have to land their small plane in a meadow because of thick fog. When they get out, they discover bear tracks: loud clock.

A mother and daughter write letters to each other over the course of their lives: quiet clock.

Now, I have to say that sometimes people talk about how writing has to serve readers, hook them, entertain them, pay them off, earn them, keep them from putting the book down, and I don't dispute this, but I also don't think worrying about it necessarily leads to better, more complex, richer writing. I'm not suggesting that stories need a clock because the fang-toothed overlord readers will give you a bad Goodreads review if you don't have one. My writing gets better when I think of my reader as a collaborator rather than an adversary.

Thinking about a container of time is a powerful way to engage energy. Where is the pressure coming from? Can there be more?

Key

First, name the clock as you understand it so far. Are you zoomed in very close—say, a day or two? Or is this story spread out over a long and undefined space of time?

Next, list any temporal markers or possibilities. Maybe the story starts in spring and has to wind down before the rains stop and summer dries everything out, or maybe someone is pregnant, or a child is turning ten, or two people are days away from a big wedding and one has doubts.

Now consider the ways in which time might put pressure on the events and characters. Perhaps you zero in on the twenty-four hours before the wedding, or use that pregnancy as your month-by-month frame. Sometimes simply naming the clock, no matter how loud or quiet it is, helps to put boundaries around the piece so you have something to push against.

Very often, narrowing the field of time helps to make a story move. It helps to eliminate repetitive scenes and to give you, the writer, permission to make moments interesting, present, or immediate because they are singular. If your book takes place over the course of a single week, then every day has to be different from every other day.

DOORWAY #52

Sign Your Own Permission Slip

What Would You Do with a Hall Pass?

When we talk about writer's block, usually it has to do with a fear of being judged. The voice inside my head says the idea is stupid, the approach won't work, one decision is good and one decision is bad and I won't know which is which until it's too late. It feels like there is a high school hall monitor in my brain and every movement is a no-no. The hall monitor is telling me that I can't go to the bathroom right now, that I'm not supposed to slam my locker, that I need to quiet down while walking with my friends. She doesn't like the pins on my jacket or the color of my hair.

A book I'll admire and love forever is *The Book of Delights* by Ross Gay. It is composed of a year's worth of mini essays, one each day, each about something that delights Gay. Delights include bringing a tomato seedling on an airplane, the beauty of nicknames, of babies, of cancer remission, of public toilets. It insists on joy against and in the midst of losses and a hard world. *The Book of Delights* is decidedly not a project predicated on anyone else's permission. It had to be Gay himself saying yes to each day's attempt, to the contours of his interest and attention, to finding his own personal delight and putting it up to the light.

It is in this spirit that I hand out actual permission slips to my writing classes so that everyone can literally become their own signatory. It feels weirdly exhilarating to watch a room full of young writers mark it down that way, on paper, and sign on the dotted line. Giving yourself permission is a little bit bratty and a little bit bossy, and sometimes that's exactly what we need.

To Whom It May Concern:
Ramona Ausubel has permission to put a living woolly mammoth in her novel.
Thanks for supporting this attempt!
Ramona Ausubel

Key

If you want to write, you must become the anti–hall monitor. Run out the double doors in the middle of algebra holding your self-signed permission slip high. Take the barriers and make them into slides.

- Permission to write toward joy.
- Permission to do a deep dive into your lifelong interest in block-printed linens.
- Permission to start a novel even though you don't know how to write a novel (yet).

- Permission to try writing in the second person.
- Permission to write the essay in the form of a recipe.
- Permission to write about your mother.
- Permission to be slow to respond to all noncritical emails for three months while you focus on writing.

Now sign with your biggest, boldest pen and get to work.

DOORWAY #53

Do the Next Most-Interesting Thing

More Volcanoes, More Islands

I wrote the islands. I wrote what I knew or wanted to know so far. Green dots of land in the sea of what was still unwritten or unseen.

I now have an archipelago of prose. I have a bit about the father's childhood and a bit about the brothers in elementary school and a section that takes place in the future and a whole bunch of little moments involving various dogs. What now?

I'll begin by reading the whole thing. Very importantly, I need to enter this reading having had a chat with myself about grace. I remind myself that I wrote with the understanding that I was following my nose, following what felt present, and that my reader self needs now to be gentle and kind. I absolutely cannot go into this with a red pen or a suspicious heart. In fact, this read is not about assessing quality in any way! I will make NO EDITS. I'm reading for connections and opportunities only. I'm going to keep a list as I go.

By way of example, here are a few of my real notes from the read I did at this stage for the novel I'm currently working on:

That scene where Mom talks about falling while hiking echoes the moment the older son tweaks his back chopping wood. Mortal bodies—more to explore.

So much sibling love in teenage parts! Look for what happens to that later on.

Swimming is a release and a source of power for the first half. It gets more complicated when S is being coached by B. He's changed swimming for her. Explore the way he takes ownership of the thing she used to love. Reclaiming that is important in the last act.

There's good stuff about building the house—more construction. More effort to find shelter.

Shelter! Is that what the whole thing is about? Water is a kind of shelter for S. His house is shelter for B, until the fire threatens it. What's Mom's shelter?

How is loneliness answered in the last act?

There is a lot of New Mexico landscape in the first half, but when S goes to California the only landscape is water. Draw a sharper line around this stark shift.

Key

Print your piece or gather all of your handwritten pages. Set it on your lap. Feel the weight of what you have made so far. Remind yourself that you did this work by trusting your gut, that it is a new life and only needs your love and attentive eye right now.

As you read, keep a running list of observations and connections. Notice everything.

Once you have read the whole thing and thought about all those connections, begin another journey of island writing and island connecting. Sometimes this might feel similar to that first island draft where new blips of land pop up out of the deep blue. Sometimes it feels like expanding one of the islands already present. Sometimes you'll build a bridge between two spits of land. Sometimes it's more like writing the topography beneath the surface. As in the earlier attempt, follow your nose and trust in the wisdom of what you understand or feel connected to right now.

DOORWAY #54

Body Map

Locating Emotion in the Skin and Skeleton

In the last week I have felt my chest tighten with anxiety about standing in front of a new group of students to make a space where we all feel brave enough to write. As I type this, I still have threads of pain from a migraine that melted my brain three days ago, which also reminded me (again, again) that I am a mortal creature. My fingers keep reaching for the phone to check the status of wildfires surrounding many people I love. A piece of good writing news made me feel a by-now-familiar combination of shame and happiness. This specific shame is almost soft, like a blanket draped over my shoulders. I know it well. I have learned to expect it when good things happen. This happens in my body, and my body tells the story of a moment in my life.

As in many other spheres, creative writing discussions can compartmentalize ideas or truths that are deeply entwined. We talk about "backstory" like it is a separate block that can be thonked down to explain why the boyfriend is being such a jerk right now (his dad was a jerk to him, see?). We talk about "emotional complexity" like it's one item on a checklist in which we need to demonstrate that the jerky boyfriend also has a soft side—see him there drinking lemon tea and looking at kittens on the internet? We discuss "characterization" and "interiority." All of these are useful terms, sometimes.

And yet I never (seriously, never) set out to *do* them because this language is not how I experience being alive in all its heartbreak and beauty and helplessness and love, or any of the other sources from which I write. Being alive is happening within me and around me. In some way, it's all happening at once. Memory is a swirl and a carousel and we're all walking around thinking about things in the past, which folds those events into the present. We carry generations of trauma and memory in our genetic code. Mothers continue to house the cells of their babies in their bodies for the rest of their lives. We are full of scars and hearts made both stronger and heavier with love.

Body mapping is a therapeutic tool used to reflect on and represent lived experiences by visualizing the places in the body where trauma, joy, pleasure, loss, uncertainty, and past experiences dwell. I love this tool for getting to know a character (real or imagined) because it is about the meeting points of infinite layers of experience. The physical and the emotional, the imaginary and the real, the body as home and as site of alienation, as history and as future, as location of pain and pleasure. The body (which includes the mind and the heart) is the place from which all else is experienced. It is our ultimate setting.

Key

Draw a map of a character's body, indicating the places where the past is housed, the spots where fear and hope live. Where in the body does this character carry the people they worry about and love? Name the physical realities that are always or sometimes present. Name the generational or historical or inherited peculiarities, struggles, weights, powers, gifts. Where does shame live and what is its texture? When this character thinks of a key event from your piece, what happens inside them? Where are the secrets?

You might focus on one moment or a character over their lifetime.

DOORWAY #55

Flora and Fauna

What Else Is Alive Here?

Characters—the human lives in a story—take up most of my page space and brain space. I think about who everyone is and the old questions: What do they want? What do they think they want? What is standing in their way? I think about what inner ache would motivate a certain action. Then there's the whole architecture of plot and how every decision relates to every other decision and if there's going to be a scene where the child throws a potato at the neighbor then are we also going to need a scene where the dad buys the potatoes and why is the kid so mad and is the neighbor a jerk or maybe the neighbor is really nice which scares the kid for some essential and undetermined reason . . . oof. Decisions are a lot. Sometimes it feels like my story arms are so full of decisions and questions about character and plot that I can't hold anything else.

This is a very good time to set all of that down on a nice soft surface and turn my attention toward the more-than-human world.

I recently invited my university's bug zoo to visit one of my creative writing classes. At first my students were confused.

Bugs? Creative writing? We met a rosy tarantula and some hissing cockroaches and saw beautiful scorpions and beetles preserved in acetate. After we learned about the creatures who had come to our classroom in a big, wheeled cooler, we told bug stories. It turned out we had a *lot* to say about insects. I learned more about this group of people by way of the insects they had known, run from, smushed, been awed by than any other conversation we had had before. One woman told a story about the ladybugs that always came on the anniversary of her grandmother's death. Another talked about her relationship with the orb weaver spiders that built their nests across the path to her mailbox, which she swept clear each day, and how she felt guilty, but then the webs were back the next day. This, she said, was a lesson in meeting each day with a full heart. The stories taught me about the places where these humans lived and the six- and eight-legged creatures that lived there with them, but they also taught me what my students noticed and how observation reveals feeling and meaning. The ladybugs became a ghost of the woman's grandmother. The orb weaver spiders wove not only webs but the texture of my student's day.

Key

Set down the big architecture and decisions. Set down the major "whys" and "wherefores." Kneel in the dirt with a character and take notice of the ants. Pay attention to the bird's nest in the pine tree or the rabbit in the yard. Plant some bulbs. Prune back the wild blackberries. Lives are being lived in all the quiet spaces of your scenes and settings. Allow the characters on the page to wake to something bright or strange around them. Allow yourself to wake to something new about that person.

DOORWAY #56

Fold the Piece in Half

And Find the Echoes, Answers, or Counterparts

Here I am: I have struck out into the unknown, followed interests, threads, and glimmers. As established, the goal has been to go hunting for the most interesting stuff I can turn up or create.

I've been trying to stay awake and present, to do the next most-interesting thing, to have fun. Still, somewhere around the eighty-page mark, I often run out of gas.

This reminds me of when I studied abroad in college and the teacher said to us bright and excited Americans, "It's all new now, but after three or four weeks, the honeymoon period will end and you'll probably feel homesick and a little sad." Right on schedule, a month in, all ten of us sought the comfort of even the least convincing of bagels, felt hungry for a familiar movie in the language of our home. The known felt like a raft we might float on to catch our breath. And it did not last—soon I was back to eating street sausages at 3 a.m. and fried cheese at every other time of day and summoning my emergent Czech with every taxi driver and bartender.

If the first eighty pages are the honeymoon (maybe it's shorter—that's okay too!), then this doorway is not so much about resting on a blow-up swan made of bad bagels but about using known materials from the pages you have written so far in order to journey deeper into the draft. Here, we stand right in that crux between the first foray, in which we glimpsed the wild unknown only by the light of a headlamp, and the second, undertaken in search of order and continuity.

Key

I picture this exercise as a Rorschach test where I fold a piece of paper, pressing the freshly painted half against the unpainted half to see what shape emerges in the doubling or echo. Instead of the blob revealing my innermost secrets, the print reveals the secrets of the story I'm trying to write.

- Describe the characters as you know them so far: What do they want? What are their quiet obsessions? What are their moods? Tics?

- Describe the tone and texture of the story—the dark shadows and flashes of light.

- Describe all the settings and how they are in play so far. What is the city's character, or that of the plains or the wind?

- What questions have been posed so far? What is the black hole, as discussed in Doorway #12?

- Take note of details or small moments that stand out to you as especially energetic or alive.

- Make a small inventory of the most interesting things—objects, furnishings, talismans—in the pages so far.

- Take note of anything else that stands out or has electricity that isn't already in one of the above categories.

Now your job is to find the opposite, echo, answer, or counterpart to each of these (or many of them—you don't need to get to every single thing). What would the negative imprint of a character's initial laziness look like? Or does that initial laziness increase until it has a significant impact? If the wind blows in a ferocious way to begin with, what might it do as time goes on? Throw those questions up and see if you can imagine some answers and/or new questions born from them. Someone sits on a chair and it breaks—does that chair or its shards or the bruise from the fall come back later?

This works as well for both the half draft (where you might picture folding that foundational half upward to see what might grow from what you have written) and the islands draft (where you might print the islands you have onto the empty sea to look for new connections; for every island, find an echo, a counterpart, a shadow).

The point is not that every story can or should be symmetrical. That every question has an answer. The idea here is to use the energy and matter and intelligence of what you have already put down to move forward in a way that captures the emotional logic of this early material. This way, you don't have to start from scratch each day. Earlier you wrote the scene where the man falls to the floor when the chair splinters beneath him, and today you have something to work with. The anger or embarrassment of the man, the dark bruise on his hip, the broken chair leg he could use to . . . what?

Each line drawn between what is there now and what might be becomes a tightrope you can walk on. It's thin and it requires some balance, but it is a way across the canyon.

DOORWAY #57

The Obsession Connection

Locating Character via Idiosyncrasy, Curiosity, and Desire

Everyone is weird. Everyone has odd habits, desires, unvoiced opinions, secret interests, minor or major obsessions, things stored in the back of a drawer. Every single person in the café, in the office, in the car parked next to mine, has a full landscape of strangeness. Even if someone told you none of their usual biography (hometown, job, marital status, etc.), you would understand key parts of them if they revealed their obsessions and habits. While the biography has control and gloss, the hidden details are rough and real. What is more sincere than an unspoken secret?

Key

For each character, name:

- an obsession (maybe it's keeping the toilet clean or Irish wool sweaters or crocheting pot holders or reading NBA stats)

- three habits (a seventeen-step skin care routine, taking the neighbor's trash out, watching the same movie every Friday on mute after work)

- one unfulfilled desire (to kiss another girl, to learn to sew, to live in a big city)

What makes this person weird? What makes this person unlike the guy standing next to them in the supermarket line?

Idiosyncrasy is humanity—absolutely no one is normal. Finding your character's peculiarity will make them real. Even one secret window can bring you closer to them.

DOORWAY #58

Secrets and Desires

Your Character's Internet History Reveals All

This side quest in the "Obsession Connection" journey is useful enough to be its own doorway. I have been offering a character-building class for years, and the prompt that almost always reveals the most is to unearth and write about a character's last five Google searches. The internet is where we go to get answers to questions we don't want to ask out loud. My browser contains the trail of my distraction, the tab with a $400 hand-knit sweater from Copenhagen that I won't ever buy but leave open as a way to live with the loveliness for a few days, the flight search for a trip I'm dreaming of, a question about how to rehab a broken pinky, a guide to the rights of undocumented immigrants to keep on hand in case students need it, tips on how to help a kid with anxiety. You could know nothing else about me, but if you saw my browser history you would begin to form a picture.

In the café where I was working this morning, the woman next to me kept tabbing between her work Slack, several adoptable puppies, articles on antidepressant medications, and a YouTube channel on styling curly hair. Those searches gave me a tiny window into her life.

When I recently typed "Why is" into Google, the first results were:

"Why is my poop green?"

"Why is my wife angry at me?"

"Why is my husband angry at me?"

If that doesn't sum up our species, I don't know what does. We are so smart and capable and so small and helpless.

Key

Take a deep dive into your characters' browsing and search histories. Consider the character at any given key moment in the piece. What were their open tabs the year their mother was hospitalized? What questions did the teenage girl ask the internet in incognito mode? Our online lives reveal the breadth of our interests, so remember to capture people's desires, their hustle, their distraction, their unanswerable questions, their practical needs, their weird curiosities and temptations. What does the algorithm serve up that they always click? What does the algorithm get wrong?

Once you've gone snooping, you can choose how to incorporate this information into the piece. Maybe you describe the search history directly, or maybe we see a moment where a character looks, reads, searches. Or maybe it simply becomes background for you.

DOORWAY #59

Write Your Character's Obituary

The End Lights the Beginning

Thesis #1: The world is a very strange, beautiful, sad, and amazing place. See: There is such a thing as a platypus; a stand of aspen trees is one organism; someone right now is thinking about how war will work on Mars; someone is taking care of an orphaned elephant; someone is climbing a sheet of ice in the Himalayas. We have hundreds of mango varieties, have invented thousands of languages, have killed one another and saved one another's lives trillions and trillions of times.

Thesis #2: We go about our regular lives—we pay the car insurance, buy bread, text about the best time to meet a friend—and all the while, over the course of each of our lives, we will experience things so huge and so delicate we might never know how to explain them to ourselves or another person. We have parents who love us in tremendous or inadequate ways; we have homes that we have left and homes we have not yet been to; we will each lose the very dearest of things; we are alive on a planet in flux. Our inner lives are far outsized from our day-to-day. This is why I write fiction—it allows me a chance to restore some of that balance, to give voice to the complexity of what we each experience.

Taking that paradoxical truth, I think about a few other things when writing characters.

1. Tension: Writers are always talking about dramatic tension. Sometimes this means that there is a kind, docile father on one side and a rageful, ferocious mother on the other. Sometimes it means that the sweet old lady from the post office is a talented cat burglar. Sometimes it means that we readers watch a single woman in heels walking through a parking garage at night and we hear her shoes click and also hear the lower-pitched click of the shoes of an unseen person. In each of those examples, there are opposing forces. That is tension. If everything on the page agrees, there's no chemical reaction, no propulsion.

2. Surprise: A story that goes exactly where we expect it to is the worst kind of story. Our attention is arrested when our expectations are subverted. In Gabriel García Márquez's story "A Very Old Man with Enormous Wings" we see an angel, but instead of being luminous and lovely, he's kind of gross. His wing feathers are full of bugs, he smells terrible, and even when he tries to enact a miracle, he doesn't get it right at all. Márquez takes what we might expect from a trait or a circumstance and reverses it.

3. A way of seeing: Character is not only the person but every single thing they see. The world is different through different eyes, and different too through the same person's eyes on another day. Imagine a woman standing on a subway platform in New York City. She is twenty years old, wearing black jeans and a loose sweater, her hair in a bun. There are rats on the tracks and an old man is playing "Let It Go"

from *Frozen* on the trumpet. It's rush hour and the station is busy. Imagine that this woman is on her way to the hospital where her father is dying. How does the subway station look? How does the music sound? What does she notice about the other passengers? The smell? Now imagine that instead of going to see her dying father, the woman has heard that she got into a PhD program in microbiology at Yale and is about to quit the job she hates as a receptionist in a dentist's office. How does the subway station look now? How does the music sound? What does she notice about the smell, the other passengers?

4. Lastly, truth and meaning: It may be fiction, but it feels like the truth. The Márquez story works because it's funny and has beautiful imagery and is full of precise, surprising details, but also because it's about something real. It's about how selfish and pathetic we humans can be. If we don't see immediate gain, we might let an angel rot in the chicken coop.

As you create characters, keep in mind these elements: tension, surprise, the way the world is altered by the eyes through which it is seen, and deeper truth.

Even if I'm writing one day of a person's life (or a week, or a summer), it can be useful to fly my little writer brain to the very end of their days to see what ended up mattering most, how this person was seen, held, or remembered, and what such an end-of-life summary might leave out.

Here is an obituary I wrote for a character, seeking that wide scope.

> Effie Mack was born in Springfield, Indiana, in the middle of a tornado. Her mother was in used-car sales

> and her father was a librarian. She had seven sisters, all of them volleyball stars. Effie herself owned racehorses (her favorite, Night Doctor, won the Kentucky Derby on Effie's fortieth birthday) and married a jockey who was half her height. They never had children and retired to Argentina. They contracted dengue fever on a jungle expedition from which they never returned.

That's the biography, the outer shell. But I also want to know what was happening on the inside. You'll recognize some of the questions I ask myself from other doorways in this second paragraph of the obituary:

> All her life, Effie carried the piece of chewing gum her father had in his mouth when he died. She kept this, along with a lucky rabbit's foot gifted to her by her youngest sister, in a plastic bag in the bottom of her purse. She treasured the tiny shoes her jockey husband wore the day he won the derby and wouldn't give them away even though they were brittle and cracked. Every few weeks, Effie dreamed that she had left a window open and that a polar bear came in and ate her up. Before she died, Effie and her husband, feverish on the banks of the Amazon, watched a monkey swing through the trees and laughed at his red butt and pinched face. The last three Google searches on her computer were "Poisonous snakes of South America," "Blister prevention," and "How to save your marriage."

Any number of stories could be written about this woman. Any collection of moments could become the focus, and a short story featuring Effie might omit many of these details, but writing the two paragraphs—outer and inner lives—gives me a portrait of a life to write into and from. It also gives me a bunch of details to plant like seeds.

Key

Here are some possible details to include in the first paragraph of your character's obituary:

- Name:
- Location of birth:
- Detail or two about the birth (weather, first words mother or father said):
- Parents' lines of work:
- Number of siblings and one detail about one or more of them (notable talent, notable failure, notable physical trait):
- Character's job:
- Did they volunteer somewhere or have a hobby?
- Did they have children?

- Did they move away from home or stay close to where they were born?

- How did they die? Who was with them?

- Is there anything strange about this person's body?

And some details to add to the your second paragraph:

- Two objects they keep in their purse or pocket that aren't technically useful:

- One object they know they should give away but can't:

- A recurring dream:

- An event in the last five days that changed the character's view of the world:

- Their last three Google searches (make sure at least one of these is a question they did not want to ask out loud):

You can keep this view of a character, which is both wide-angle and as small and easy to hold as a smooth rock, with you as you write. When you need to remember who this person is, touch this stone.

DOORWAY #60

Commit to the Bit

Double Down to Root Out What You Really Want to Say

Dolly Parton said, "Find out who you are and do it on purpose." On *Project Runway* the judges are always asking aspiring fashion designers about the point of view of their clothes and the way a collection tells a story. Comedy is often funny because it pushes an idea—a "what if"—past the point of mild discomfort. All of these are lessons in committing to the bit. The absurd is perhaps the most bit-committed genre, but even if you don't want to write literature of the absurd, it's useful to see, in an almost cartoonish way, how far an idea can be taken. When I stretch an idea all the way to its furthest extreme, I often realize how far I have been toward the opposite end—the safer-feeling end of uncommitted.

It makes sense to begin with a "maybe," with a "what if." To poke my nose over the windowsill of an idea. To sketch something in pencil so faint it could be erased in one easy swipe if the idea was deemed silly.

There's a lie in this feeling of safety. Something can be a "maybe" or a "what if" for only so long. The more I hedge, the smaller my voice becomes.

Key

Read a scene or a chapter or a story with this question in mind: Where have I not committed? Sometimes this happens when a character thinks about doing something rather than doing it. If June considers calling her old babysitter, with whom she was slightly in love, would it be more interesting if she actually picked up the phone? Sometimes the lack of commitment comes in the form of a character being soft around the edges, a little neutral. If so, think about how you can push that person to be more uncomfortable, more active, angrier or sadder or louder or weirder.

The early toe-dip into an idea is a great way to start. Once you've written onward, it's time to put your whole body in the water. Remember that, as with all things, you can always pull back later. You can always find a middle ground. For now, your job is to fully and unembarrassedly commit to the bit. Go all the way. Double the recipe. Put a small element under the microscope and make it huge.

DOORWAY #61

Picking Up the Half Draft

Write into the Spaces

After I wrote my first half-draft novel, which was the initial crack at what became my third novel, *The Last Animal*, I wondered if I might find a similarly freeing but efficient way to pick up the second draft. Since the first draft was purposefully thin, this next stage was as much generative as it was revision.

Here's what I did: I gave myself two weeks to work on each chapter. On day one of the first week, I read the chapter twice and circled on the page anywhere I wanted to add something—a new scene or a more developed scene, some backstory, a richer sense of the character. For the rest of that week I wrote into the chapter. No revision, no reading ahead, just adding to the thread count, using the information and understanding I now had after having written a beginning, middle, and end of the draft.

On day one of week two, I again read everything over twice, and this time I made notes about aspects that felt choppy, unsteady, out of order, and so on. This week felt much more like real revision. I moved things around, I worked on sentences and images, I chose between two similar metaphors, I tried to clarify and refine characters' actions and intentions scene by scene.

I found this combination of the two weeks with very different goals to be comforting and kind of . . . cozy? The timing struck the right pace: too fast to overthink but slow enough to settle into. Like I had a little place to hang out with this one chapter, and time to both fill it up and fill it in and then, when I was fully in the world of those pages, to sharpen and shape it. In that second week of more analytical, pattern-seeking, clarifying work, I had become an expert on that chapter.

When it was time to move on to my two-week date with the next chapter, the one I'd worked on had come a long distance. It felt not half draft anymore, but full.

Over the stretch of this draft, I came to an understanding of the novel that was broad but also quite intimate. I had invested a lot of weeks, but the effort had been structured in such a way that I had not been swimming in time. There was no room for doubt, only for continuation.

A second draft is like a high-needs toddler—it requires a ton of attention and wants everything you have to give and more (Now cookies! Now nap! Now blocks! Now books! Now swings! Now water! Hug me! Don't touch me! Crackers! Crackers! Crackers!)—so it can be helpful to draw some lines around what you'll work on, when. You cannot work on everything at once (at least I can't—maybe you are some kind of super-genius!). Without parameters, it's easy to skip across the surface of a project endlessly without knowing how to settle in.

A first draft, especially a half draft, is not fully formed, even though it has a lot of core material. Giving yourself dedicated space for growth can open the project to new moments and connections that probably would not have come if you were only in revision, refinement, pattern-making mode.

Key

When I used this system, my novel had something like fifteen chapters, so thirty weeks of work fit my academic calendar perfectly. Two weeks is arbitrary, though. Maybe you have longer chapters or you like to move more slowly. Maybe you have tons of short chapters or vignettes and want to move more quickly. Think about your own brain, your own creative process, and your own real life. As ever, an ambitious but realistic pace is the magic combination because you see significant progress without burning yourself out too quickly. As always, build in space for interruptions and breaks.

An alternative to the two-week structure I used is to continuously write into the chapters, one after the next (one per week, or whatever timing fits your rhythm), and then switch to the revision at the same pace. If that's what feels right, do that. Both kinds of attention are key, but the exact approach should be your own.

Whatever the particulars of the calendar you set, make the rhythm simple and easy to follow. The work will always be hard, which is why a clear system for writing is such a gift.

DOORWAY #62

Hermit Crab

One Life Inside the Shell of Another

In their seminal book on writing creative nonfiction, *Tell It Slant*, Brenda Miller and Suzanne Paola coined the term "hermit crab essay" for a piece of writing inside the shell of another form: a transcript, a crossword puzzle, a recipe, a postpartum depression scale, and so forth. I love adopting and adapting form, even though I don't write many essays. Luckily, the method works as well for fiction. The short story I wrote about the Cyclops looking for love on the internet took the form of a step-by-step guide on how to write a successful online dating profile.

In the story I adopted the impossibly cheery voice of the internet guide and offset it with the increasingly honest and darker voice of the Cyclops. That tension made the story much more fun to write and much more interesting than it would have been if I had had only the Cyclops's sections. There's something freeing about taking on an existing shape and set of expectations and choosing where to follow and where to break. Having something to push against is easier than having total freedom.

I wrote the Cyclops story without expecting anything to come of it. I was working on a novel at the time and I needed a break and a little bit of weird, sharp-edged fun. I liked the story and I sent it to my agent, and to my absolute surprise, it wound up in the pages of *The New Yorker*. If I had set out to write a story for that magazine, I *never* would have chosen a sarcastic online dating piece about a mythical dude. I would have tried something serious, something timely, something that reached toward intellectual heights. There are so many lessons in this: The weird, fun, playful thing is often the one that sails farthest; don't try to predict what someone else will want—write what *you* want the best way you can and then go looking for a home for that piece; the side project has a life of its own.

My colleague Sarah Perry wrote a memoir about her mother's murder, which happened when Sarah was twelve years old. It is an excellent, devastating book. After it was published, she was working on a kind of sequel and it was hard and dark and complicated, so she started a secret project of mini essays about candy. She did not expect that anyone would ever want to see a book of essays about candy, but she loved writing it. At some point, she let this fact slip to her editor, who said, "The secret project is always good. Send it to me when you're done." That book, *Sweet Nothings*, came out in 2025, and it is not only joyful and weird but full of depth.

Key

Look in your current project for places to develop hidden forms. A legal brief in the middle of a divorce story, say. Step aside from the scenes and current action of the piece and write a cousin to the text that works on its own. Maybe this ends up being part of the story, or maybe it's a nice break that gives you some fresh insight. Maybe it ends up being a semi-related stand-alone.

Or: Step aside from your current work and have a brief, consequence-free affair with something weird and altogether new. Even if this has absolutely nothing to do with The Big Project, new oxygen will enter your lungs and you'll have fun.

Here is a very small list of possible forms to hermit crab into, some of them drawn from a longer list in the anthology *The Shell Game*, edited by Kim Adrian (there are some excellent essays in that book, too, if you become inspired to study the form).

- wedding vows
- questionnaire
- order form
- résumé
- natural history
- birth certificate
- year-end report
- hunting permit
- playlist

- do-it-yourself exorcism guide
- missed connections ad
- victim impact statement
- pawn ticket
- corporate memo
- middle school yearbook
- public apology letter

Obviously, you can invent your own!

Part 3

Doorways Up: Getting Perspective

DOORWAY #63

Your Novel/Story in Images

A Visual Outline

Among the most pressing questions we all have, along with Do you believe in God? What happens when you die? and What the eff should I cook for dinner? is: Do you outline?

I do keep a kind of outline going, like a shifting map of the geography of the book, and it helps me in a logical way. I need the timeline and the people's ages at various points and other facts and figures. But when I'm having a hard time holding the book in my mind all at once (i.e., always), something that really helps me see it again is to write, in a few sentences each, a handful of prevailing images across the span of the piece. I have these for the beginning, middle, and end, but you can do more—six or eight—for more texture. This also helps for figuring out a chapter. What are some images that remind me of what matters here? Images that capture the feeling that everything else should be building toward? There are a lot of words in a novel. This is a way to keep a clear picture of what all of them are supposed to be working for.

Here are three from *The Last Animal*, to give you a sense of what I'm talking about (spoiler alert).

1. Beginning image: Two sisters, Vera and Eve, ages thirteen and fifteen, sit on a pile of bones their scientist mother has helped excavate from melting permafrost. The girls drink their mother's vodka and imagine mall air-conditioning.

2. Middle image: A baby mammoth has been born via gene editing and an Asian elephant mother in a private zoo in Italy, but the mammoth is not well and she is noisy and sad. The younger daughter hangs a white sheet on a laundry line in the mammoth's enclosure and projects movies of the Pleistocene Epoch onto it to try to calm the animal. The three women and the mammoth all watch together.

3. End image: After an escape, after coming to understand that this animal cannot live in this time and should not be asked to, the scientist mother and her daughters drive into the Alps, find a dense forest, walk several hours in, and watch as the mammoth walks away into the forest.

Unlike a typical outline, which is all procedures and events, this is about the heartbeat. Every time I picture those three images, I remember again what this story is about for me, what those sections are about. I remember the soul of this book so I can keep writing toward that.

Key

This works as well for a chapter or other smaller section as it does for a whole book. Start by writing (or identifying, from existing material) a prevailing image in each major section of the book; or, if you are stuck on a smaller section, say a middle chapter, try the same exercise only for those pages. You could also have a single image that encapsulates the feeling of the whole project.

If you want, try drawing these images and tacking them above your writing space. It doesn't matter if the drawings are good (mine are not!); it's just nice to look at them and be reminded in one glance of what you are writing toward.

DOORWAY #64

Opposites

Building Tension in Hidden Places

If I want to make the most of dramatic tension (that line stretched tight between two poles), then I need opposing forces in my work. This goes beyond the usual idea of conflict.

I want as much tug in my story as possible, and I can get it from landscape, character, situation, inventory, plot, language—everything. Think of the way humor and sadness work against and with each other. Let's say my setting is a rain forest, lush and green and dense. Something then needs to be set in opposition to that—emptiness, drought, thirst.

I make a list of what I consider the ten or twenty most important aspects of my story. Objects, places, emotional states, situations, wants, themes. I consider what's pulling at or against each one. Some of them may already oppose one another, but I might see that some of my elements are flapping in the breeze. I need to tie that line off somewhere else and pull it tight. A post in the ground is a post in the ground, but if there's something tugging at it, it becomes active. Whatever the pole marks—a kind of loneliness, a wish for love, a wish for justice, a place where a father tripped and fell, a memory of war, a mountain range—it is energetic. This is tension. This propels us. The question is partly about which side will pull more strongly, if there will be a winner, but it's also about the note that each of those taut lines makes when you strike it. The line between father and mother sounds a singular note. The line between the heart-thirsty sailor and the rain forest sounds a singular note.

Key

Go through your manuscript (or the idea in your head) and make a list of elements that have energy of any kind. They can be objects, character traits, settings, kinds of weather, language, or tone—truly anything. Start with ten so that it's not too overwhelming, but feel free to keep going. Let's say you have a girl who is furious with her father for reading her journal. For me, fury and a breach of trust are energetic. Now we need an opposite. What if this discovery occurs on a beautiful, perfect summer evening with fireflies and warm, gentle air? The rest of the family is sitting outside laughing over a game of gin, and the girl can hear their joyful voices rise into the evening. Not only do we have the fury over the breach of trust, but the whole world seems to be refuting the girl's anger by being so lovely she almost can't stand it.

Make sure each element you have named has an opposite in tone, texture, image, idea, or situation.

DOORWAY #65

Retype

In Order to Revise, Start Again

Several years ago, I polled a lot of writer friends about their most useful revision tips. The one that came in most frequently and with the most religious zeal was to retype from the first word, revising along the way. Laura van den Berg said, "Apart from dogs, I am a giant fan of retyping once you hit the stage where you feel the rough shape is right, but still need to do a good bit of reimagining and have no idea how to set about it. I keep the original doc next to me as I retype, revising along the way. This might sound tedious—and sometimes it *is* tedious; retyping is also a great litmus test for what needs to be cut—but it amazes me how many new doors open when the page is blank once more."

Lauren Groff famously writes a draft of a novel longhand, recycles it *without reading*, and then starts again. I will never be that tough and I think Lauren must have a better memory than I do, but the principle of a second beginning stands.

A huge and critical truth is that revision does *not* mean polishing. It means undoing, reimagining, reversing, flipping, opening up. This strategy asks us to consider again each and every line rather than skimming over while reading.

Key

Print what you have and set it on the desk beside you. Open a fresh document and begin to retype from the hard copy. Your goal is to go slowly, to listen to sentences and change them so they feel and sound right. Add new lines, move pieces around. Adjust images. Rewrite dialogue. Let the retyping become a generative process of its own. All the writers who recommended this assured me that what seems like a much slower process is far more efficient because the draft will be deeper and the changes greater than if you simply tinker. When you finish this new draft, you will have come a significant distance.

DOORWAY #66

The Five Whys

An Unexpected Use of a Corporate Productivity Exercise

When engineers at Toyota, the car company, run into a problem, the protocol is to ask "the five whys" in order to get to the root of the issue. The method was described by Taiichi Ohno, the engineer who developed Toyota's production system, and the company still uses it today. Toyota has a "go and see" philosophy. This means that decisions are based on walking down to the factory floor or doing other discovery to understand what's actually going on, rather than relying on boardroom theories of what might be going on.

The method is simple. After identifying a problem or sticking point:

1. Ask, Why is that?

2. Ask, Why is that?

3. Ask, Why is that?

4. Ask, Why is that?

5. Ask, Why is that?

Maybe there's a bottleneck in the step where the tailpipe is attached and it's slowing everything else down. The instinctive solution might be to yell at the worker on the step and tell them to hurry. But is that really why the backlog has occurred? Probably not. In my highly sophisticated knowledge of auto factories, here's how it might look.

Problem: tailpipe attachment slowdown.

1. Why is that? Because the worker has to drill six screws and it takes forty-five seconds instead of the thirty seconds it takes the person at the previous step and the step after.

2. Why is that? Because each screw needs to be picked up by hand.

3. Why is that? Because there is no automated screwdriver arm at this step.

4. Why is that? Because it's expensive to install one.

5. Why is that? Because it needs to attach to the hooby-dooby vacuum by way of a dogleg weez.

Now the bosses can compare the cost of the constant bottleneck with the cost of installing the automated screwdriver (or possibly fixing the issue of the dogleg weez, which honestly sounds like something they really should deal with).

In the repeated questions, the team pushes past the surface issue (and, as a result, the surface-level, Scotch tape solution).

But you are not here to build a midrange reliable family sedan! Why on earth am I telling you about this?

I have used it in two ways, both helpful.

Key #1

"Five whys" your way to a story-level issue. That's what I did when I was struggling with a problem in my novel *The Last Animal*. For many drafts, the story was about a mom and dad and their two teenage daughters. The problem was that the dad was not that interesting. Here's how I figured out what to try:

Problem: Dad is not interesting.

1. Why is that? Because the story is not really about him (it's about Jane—the mom—and the girls).

2. Why is that? Because this novel is about a moment when Jane has to step out of the shadow of the men in her life and make her own mistakes and choices.

3. Why is that? Because she has been hiding in the cover of her husband's career, whereas the current project is her own.

4. Why is that? Because the world has changed (climate) and she can't be comfortable anymore.

5. Why is that? Because the idea of choosing an easy path (following her husband's career and being his shadow) was a kind of lie.

Now I had this clear picture: Earlier in her life she was the shadow and he was the life force. In this novel, in this portion of her life, she is the force and he is the shadow.

The root cause of the husband's inability to develop beyond a flat, shadowlike character was that the story was not about his being alive but about Jane's path to living and working beyond the cover he provided. Reader, I killed the dad off. In his death, one year before the novel opens, he became hugely important because he was a big, magnetic *absence*. He had been the patriarchal umbrella that Jane and her daughters had hidden under, and now the world was different and their lives were different and they didn't have shelter anymore. They were out in the weather.

Key #2

I also love this exercise for getting to the bottom of a character's motivation or essential nature.

Problem/situation: Maggie is super angry.

- Why is that? She hasn't slept in three days.
- Why is that? Her upstairs neighbor is playing trumpet dirges all night long.
- Why is that? Maggie doesn't know (therefore neither do we).
- Why is that? She is afraid to speak directly to her neighbor and also afraid to get him in trouble.
- Why is that? The neighbor is a recluse and she worries about him.

Stories don't actually want solutions because solutions (resolutions) are boring, so instead of trying to get the neighbor to be quiet so Maggie can get a good night's sleep, you are looking for ways to follow the feeling or problem toward an interesting event.

Maybe Maggie, in her sleepless fury, bakes the neighbor a lemon cake and goes bravely upstairs to deliver it with a note asking him to stop trumpeting at night, but since she's a little afraid of him, she knocks on the door and runs away. But he answers before she's gone and they have a conversation. You might "why" your way to the core of the neighbor's situation (maybe his cat recently died, or maybe he is practicing for a major concert at Carnegie Hall, or maybe he's going to play for his long-lost sister's wedding) and then keep asking questions to see how these characters might change each other's life in some small or big way.

DOORWAY #67

Structure as Ecosystem

Story as Floodplain, as Marsh, as Desert Mesa

Every spring my family takes a river trip on the Colorado River for three nights. We load rafts with sleeping bags and tents and camp chairs and huge jugs of water and food and every possible snack option (this is my primary role on the boat: snack lady) and float from Fruita, Colorado, past the Utah border. At first, the river is wide and the banks soft with pale green grass and mud. By the end of the first day, we enter Horsethief Canyon, which has light sandstone walls bedazzled with the nests of cliff swallows. On river right there are grassy flats where we once saw a black bear drinking from a shallow eddy. Farther on, the canyon walls stretch high and red on both sides. I like to lie on the front of the boat and look at the strata of rock reaching hundreds of feet up to the blue sky. The river has carved our path deeper into geological time, from the soft dirt of the present to the black of Precambrian granite formed 1.8 billion years ago.

A river canyon is the narrative structure of time itself. Time as layers, the earth forming and building, water carving a path over its own long course. The river itself is a story—it begins small and high and follows a path that is never straight but always logical. The twists of the story move around boulders, cliff walls, wind. Resistance shapes everything, as forward energy shapes everything.

In her wonderful book *Meander, Spiral, Explode*, Jane Alison writes, "For centuries there's been one path through fiction we're most likely to travel—one we're actually told to follow—and that's the dramatic arc: a situation arises, grows tense, reaches a peak, subsides. . . . But something that swells and tautens until climax, then collapses? Bit masculo-sexual, no?" Alison suggests that instead of always having to summit a mountain and descend changed and awakened, we can widen our narrative possibilities to include such shapes as a winding river, a series of wavelets, a firework, a cellular structure. There are infinite shapes in the world, so why shouldn't there be infinite shapes for stories or essays?

While I lie on the warm rubber of the raft with my dog on my chest, the cliffs and land are the backstory and the river is the present moment. The Colorado is so thick with silt—matter carried from upstream—that it cannot easily be filtered. The story carries the past. The story is thick with all it holds.

Key

Look inside the piece you are writing for natural phenomena or elements already present. If the story is set in a high mountain town during winter, maybe the snow banked up around the house suggests a story shape. Look at a dogwood tree, an acorn, leathery kelp stalks, the lace of ice on the windshield in the morning.

You might find a shape or structure for the whole project or for one scene. As with all things, the point is to open toward something, not to stick to it perfectly. It's more than okay if your dogwood-flower shape outgrows itself or shifts. What is more natural than evolution?

DOORWAY #68

Structure as Balance

Alexander Calder's Mobiles

My second novel is about a family that fractures when they discover that all their money (once plentiful) is gone. Mom goes on a cross-country road trip with a giant, Dad tries to sail to Bermuda with a pretty lady, and both think the other is at home with the children, who have moved into a tepee in their backyard in Cambridge, Massachusetts. The book is about each of these three legs of the family, but it's also, importantly, about whether they will be whole ever again. What is the whole when the material of existence has gone?

I kept struggling to put the pieces together in their separateness. It felt like three different books. In the middle of this process, I had a few extra hours on a trip to Los Angeles, so I went to the Los Angeles County Museum of Art. One of the exhibits was a collection of Alexander Calder's mobiles. Calder was a modern artist whose paintings and prints of bold shapes in primary colors feel both enlivening and familiar. The mobiles follow the same principle: primary colors or black and white, simple shapes.

That day, I stood before one mobile for a long time. It had a black circle on one side with three spokes leading outward to three smaller semicircles in red, blue, and yellow. It hung in absolute balance. As it turned ever so slightly in the air, shadows of the four shapes tracked across the white wall.

I suddenly understood that this was the shape of my novel. The idea or question of the family as a whole was the dark anchor, and each member (with the kids as a group) was a smaller circle. The whole was made up of the three separate groups, and apart from them. It held each person up, but it also had them trapped. The dark circle kept every satellite from drifting too far. The book was about relationships, but it was also about relationship: the distance between bodies, between hearts, between minds. The way people can be close with one another while sometimes being at a great physical distance, and the way people can be at a great emotional distance, while being in the same bed.

Once I *felt* this balance, I could conceive the structure. On the page, it looked like short chapters of each journey anchored by chapters about the family as a whole—historical and present.

Key

The mobile is a perfect form because it can be divided into any number of shapes and sent in all directions, but it must always be designed such that each part holds the others steady. No single piece can take over, even if one element is larger than the others.

Look at some pictures of Calder's mobiles, but don't stop there. See if you can find a mobile that feels close to the piece you are writing. If not, sketch something.

Maybe you build the mobile so you can see exactly how the balance works. Sticks or cut pieces of cardboard and some fishing line work well, but you can use anything you've got around.

Having thought about the physical shapes, consider now how this translates to the page. Think about relationship. Think about balance. The way one element or character is held by another.

Your work contains moving parts, which may shift as you continue to learn it better. Keep playing.

DOORWAY #69

Deep Cuts

Find the Center by Trimming

Because I have been saying yes to everything that walks in the door and making messes and writing at speed, my stories arrive at the second or third draft a little (a lot) feral. They are rangy. They are overgrown. One of my jobs at this stage is to figure out what this *thing* even is. The theory behind this doorway is that the *thing*, the *there*, is often present, if buried, and can be revealed by carving away.

Michelangelo supposedly said that in order to carve an angel out of marble, one simply had to remove all the parts of the stone that were not angel. So simple! Thanks, pal! I do really like this image, though.

Sometimes a deep cut becomes the new working draft (meaning it was a success and there is nothing from the "Cuts" draft that I want back), but often it's more of an exercise in revealing the skeleton on which I still want to add (back, or write anew) flesh and skin. In either case, it's valuable.

I like this exercise because I get to see what I love in a piece, what feels essential, and I get to feel productive by moving the parts that are less clear over to a temporary new home. Every cut is a win. Every reveal is a win.

My hunk of marble absolutely never looks like an angel by the end of this process, which is why I am not a legendary Renaissance artist. Luckily, I live in modern times and I can hot-glue the fleshy bits back on until it looks how I want it to.

Key

Save As to create a fresh start and avoid the risk of losing anything.

Read the whole thing back so you remember what you wrote and have an immediate sense of the work.

Set a goal so that you know how severe the cut wants to be. The more obtuse the draft, the sharper the cut. For me it's always at least 25 percent but often closer to 50 percent. Your goal is to reveal what is hidden. To keep the lines, paragraphs, images, and scenes that are core to the project. To move what is less clearly part of it out of the way, for now.

Everything that gets cut goes in a separate document called something like "Fish Story Cuts." It's not going away; it's in a holding place.

Once you have hit your percentage goal, read the new version. Spend some time taking notes on the skeleton you have revealed: What seems sturdiest, most able to hold the weight of whatever you end up putting back on? Are there skeletal features that are missing? New structural possibilities you now understand?

DOORWAY #70

Skeleton and Skin

Feeding the Bones

I am now in possession of a skeleton document. And I've spent some real time observing that skeleton, learning as much as I can about what the recent deep cut reveals about my story and what the story seems to want to be (or what I want it to become). It's important to note that the skeleton on the page is not necessarily the one I'll build upon—it may have shown me that what's here is wonky and off-kilter, but I now understand what shape I want to try to move toward. If that is the case, then the next step is to rewrite the skeleton itself until it feels more or less right. It does not need to be perfect, but it should be stable and sturdy and at least generally contain the core of my idea.

I am also in possession of a document with the matter and material that I removed for the deep cut. This, at least some of it, will probably go back onto the body in a considered way.

In the process of rereading the skeleton and the cuts, I always have ideas about new scenes or moments I want to write.

Key

Follow these steps to understand your skeleton and how you want to build the flesh and muscle onto it.

- Name the bones. Read the skeleton draft and write notes about the core elements, truths, concerns, and moments. This is a way to see the skeleton at a glance, rather than having to read the whole piece every time.
- Read the "Cuts" document and make a catalogue of everything that's there. This is a taxonomy of scenes, moments, and backstory.
- Mark the items on the taxonomy that you think you want to build back in. Mark the items that you do not at this moment know what to do with.
- Make a list of scenes, moments, ideas, or concerns that feel undeveloped, underdeveloped, or missing.

You now have a way to see at a glance what you're trying to do, some material to build back in in a new way, and a list of missing pieces. Time to make your monster, Dr. Frankenstein!

DOORWAY #71

The Song Experiment

What Goes in the Mother's Solo or the Uncle's Ballad?

Somewhere in the depths of the pandemic I watched a short-lived TV show called *Song Exploder* about how songwriters work. One episode was about Lin-Manuel Miranda and the writing of "Wait for It," which is Aaron Burr's ballad in *Hamilton.* Miranda talks about the way he came to know Burr by finding him in this song. How he was walking to a party in Brooklyn when the hook became clear and he voice-recorded it so it wouldn't disappear. Everything about Burr grows out of this song. And Burr's song has to be in direct opposition—texturally, energetically, in its sound—from Alexander Hamilton's song, "My Shot."

I am a deeply unmusical person, but I love the clarity and absoluteness of "getting" a character in one three-minute song. Like catching a firefly in a jar and being able to use that to light the path from then on.

I imagined songs for the characters in a story I was working on at the time. One song was a kind of sad-white-boy indie ballad probably written in a cabin in Michigan in midwinter; one was a bouncy pop-punk anthem about swimming naked. I couldn't write the actual music, but I could imagine the sound and the way it made me feel. I could hum a hook or sing a few verses. I could even imagine a scene or two from the videos. When I went back to the manuscript, I tried to infuse the energy of the songs into the characters and use that to animate them.

Key

Choose two or three of your central characters and, for each of them, imagine the song that would most completely represent who they are and what they want. Get the sound first—is this an eighties hair-band anthem with an indulgent guitar solo or a wispy singer-songwriter dirge played on a harp? Does it make you want to jump and shake your head in a dark club, or is it more of a sit-on-a-stained-velvet-couch-in-a-coffee-shop sort of vibe? See if you can write the hook. Notice how the songs oppose or contradict or work with one another. How does the way one character's "music" is expressed make another character feel? If this is fun and helpful, write some verses. If you've got more musical talent than I do, record it on GarageBand or in a voice memo. Every time you need to make a choice about what this character would do or how they would show up in a scene, recall the song.

DOORWAY #72

Map of the Heart

Cartography of the Emotional Terrain

Maps lead us from one place to another. They show us the way in, the way out, the dark woods, and the mermaid lagoon. We can map anything—the path home, the houses of our childhood friends, the route blood takes back to the heart, the terrain of a loss. Not only are stories their own kind of map and we writers all cartographers, but maps can be a tool to see a piece of writing as it emerges.

In his book *The Power of Maps*, Denis Wood writes, "No map can show everything. Could it, it would . . . *no more than reproduce the world*, which, without the map . . . *we already have.* It is only its *selection* from the world's overwhelming richness that justifies the map."

This is why we hunger for an outline. It is impossible to hold the overwhelming richness of a book all at once. It's also the reason a simple plot outline always fails me: because events without feelings don't mean that much. "Man stands on roof of car with boom box" is a visual. "Man stands on roof of car with boom box, professing his love" is a story.

Key

Get out a blank piece of paper. Imagine this field of white as the emotional lands of your piece. Now, start marking the places of importance. Variation in terrain is key: Mark mountains (significant moments of heightened feeling), valleys (the whispered or withheld feelings), forests (dense emotional spaces), and gentle streams. Create the landforms that fit your story. You could think of this as a map you might follow from left to right, coming upon moments in the order in which they occur in the story. But you could also scatter moments in whatever way makes sense to you.

Try making a separate map for each character. You might find that one person has only mountains and no valleys, which is a useful discovery (figure out what their valleys feel like!). You might find out that two characters who seem to be at odds are experiencing similar feelings (narrative potential!).

Or they experience the same event in very different ways. It might show up on one character's map as a crashing waterfall, while on her partner's map there is only a grassy meadow and the only sound the nearly inaudible chirping of baby birds.

DOORWAY #73

Map of the Land

Cartography of the Physical Terrain

Early in a project the settings always feel blurred, like the distant horizon in a watercolor landscape painting. The setting might be a college campus or a three-story apartment building in a small American city or the remembered kitchen of a childhood home. The focus is soft with a few details sketched in. I'm writing toward the feeling of the place more than the specifics of the place.

Once the story has come more into focus, I want to map out the spaces and places. I do this not to maintain consistency (though that's good) but because the physical spaces are actors in the narrative, like the characters are.

When I was in my early twenties, I had a job working as a personal assistant for a woman who lived high in the Oakland Hills in the Bay Area. Her husband was always away on business, so the two of us were usually alone in her big house. She kept the air-conditioning on all year and I had to wear a big coat and my fingers were always stiff and numb. She was not often in a good mood—she was frustrated about the smell of her new car or because she wanted to copy a DVD and didn't know how or because her husband's consulting check had not arrived when it was expected and she needed me to cancel all her expensive plans for the week. Since I was stationed in an office at the end of a long hallway, I knew she was coming for me before she arrived. That hallway was like an instrument—*thump thump thump*—as expressive as any voice. The shape of the house, the temperature, were not incidental to the experience of that year. The hallway was a character in our little drama, and so was the air conditioner, blowing even when it was fifty degrees and raining outside. I can map my experience of that year onto those spaces. By describing the landscape, I draw up all sorts of memories about who I was at that time, the subtle shame of being at someone's beck and call, how much my body did not find comfort in the house that my boss had created to fit her needs.

Key

For each important setting, either interior or exterior, draw out a rough map. Consider the distance between rooms, where the sun comes in at different times of day. Consider the neighbors and the cars parked on the street, or the thicket of aspen saplings next to a frozen stream. All of these have the potential to be part of the orchestra. You won't necessarily put all these details in the story, but you may discover that the neighbor with the barking dog or the lacy ice on the frozen stream is more a part of the music than you realized.

You can always borrow blueprints or landscape layouts from existing spaces. When I was writing about a showpiece estate on Lake Como in *The Last Animal*, I very much enjoyed the hours I spent Google Earthing palazzos in order to build—and map—the estate and menagerie where a lot of the novel takes place.

DOORWAY #74

Map of the Movement

Cartography of the Goings-On

As discussed, most of us were taught that plot has a triangular shape: inciting incident, rising action, climax, falling action, resolution. This structure is so familiar that we know and re-create it without even trying (it's also effective and reliable and there is no shame in following the known path sometimes).

I feel slightly allergic to the word "plot." It's not because I want to write stories where nothing happens or because I'm so "literary" that I think I'm above such concerns. "Plot" as a term feels bloodless to me. It feels preordained or manufactured—plastic versus skin. This is why I like to think of "movement" or "happenings": because those seem alive and awake and organic. Movement leads to movement. Change leads to change. I am more interested in following interesting and escalating changes than I am in creating rising action that results in climax. I realize this is a linguistic side step, but the small shift has allowed me to feel more connected to the progression of my stories.

When I map the movement of a story, I first want to map what is happening, rather than press the story into a premade shape. Instead of plopping what I assume will be the highest-volume scene at the tip of the familiar pyramid, I want to investigate the volume and intensity of scenes as they currently stand.

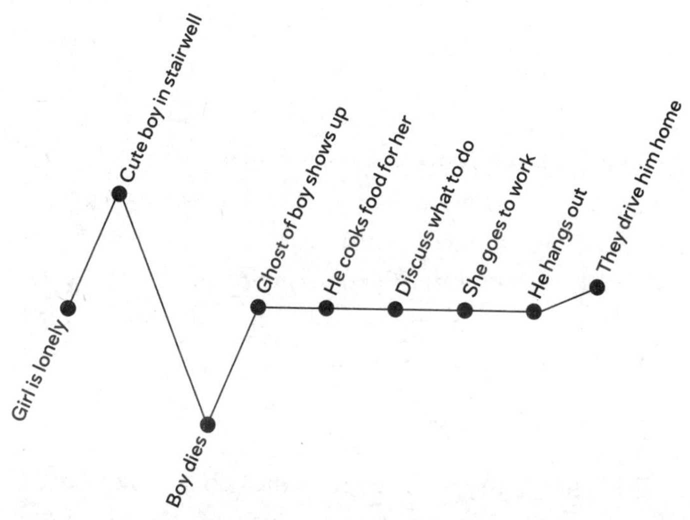

The sketch might look something like this:

Looking at this, I can see that things hit a kind of plateau. That's an opportunity to look for variation, to press one scene toward fuller, bigger expression and another toward a quieter, more introspective space.

As I go on, I keep remapping to see what has changed. Maybe I want to use at least some of the energy of that well-loved triangle. Maybe I want to break from it entirely. In either case, I have mapped and captured the energetic structure of the story as it has emerged, and can continue to sculpt either organically or by molding toward an external shape, or a combination of the two.

Key

The first choice is about how granular you want your map to be. Depending on the length of your piece, you might choose to include every scene or every chapter. If you've got a novel draft and you want to get a picture of the shape of the whole, you might choose to start with whole chapters or major scenes. If you want more detail, you can then populate scene by scene within the chapters.

Higher-tension scenes go higher on the page and lower-tension scenes go lower on the page.

Once you see what already *is*, consider how you might amplify or alter the shape so that the narrative blooms more fully. In the next draft, you'll know, for example, that a group of scenes is the calm before the storm of the explosion to come, so when you revise those, you can instill the maximum amount of pent-up energy. Or you'll know that the flashback in chapter 3 is on the same longitudinal line as the introspective moment in chapter 13, which might register as a sort of echo.

Maps are all about relationships between objects, spaces, and inhabitants. A valley is only a valley because there is a mountain range on one side. Look for relationships in the movement to bring the shape of your story into focus.

DOORWAY #75

Map of Meaning

Finding the Circles of Concern

All along in the writing process I have been naming and renaming my Black Hole to Which All Other Matter Is Drawn. The black hole has changed as the story and my understanding of the story have changed. This dead-center dot remains a navigational marker, yet the story is a bigger universe. All the themes and questions, the concerns, the reaching—these are stars in that same sky.

To understand what I am writing and to write it well, I must never lose track of the "why." Any beautiful image on the page must be beating with the about-ness of the moment. It must matter.

I have character, landscape, and movement maps, but to see the project completely, I need a map of meaning.

Key

In the middle of a piece of paper, place a dark dot and name the black hole, as you currently understand it.

Working outward from most central to least, map out the themes, questions, and concerns in the piece. Place similar ideas in clusters.

What you have in front of you is the thematic universe of your story.

Like a good astronomer, look for constellations by connecting dots.

DOORWAY #76

Map Overlay

Putting It All Together

Each map is useful for its own sake, and each provides a way to make movement and choices. In the end, the project will come together as a woven whole, not as separate threads. This is why I want to lay all my maps out together to look for connections and relationships, holes and happenings, between them.

Key

Lay all your maps side by side on a big table or on the floor. First, look between any two maps to search for connections or tension. Write your notes and observations as a list.

Next, look between the following two maps and write your notes as a list.

Mix the maps and compare crosswise (so that each has been observed with each).

Last, look at the whole picture together. Most useful at this stage might be opportunities you could explore or exploit—the emotional map shows you that you've missed writing the full extent of the tension around tidiness and motherhood, say (two themes you've got down on your meaning map). Look too for over-explored terrain that could use more variation, or places where the volume can be adjusted so that each aspect registers the way you want it to.

These lists are the driving directions to cross through to the next draft or stage. You've mapped the terrain, and now you know how to move through it again, this time with a bigger, richer understanding of the world and how it works.

DOORWAY #77

Playlist

Find the Zone with Music

In a perfect world I would have two hours of writing time first thing in the morning (with tea and scones brought on a silver tray, if you please), then time for a long hike, then another hour to write. I wouldn't turn down a nap somewhere in the afternoon, and it would be lovely if I could read for a few hours before dinner while looking out at the ocean or a meadow. These are the perfect conditions. In my life so far, I have had a total of maybe three days like this. Maybe. In the absence of this fantasy version of being a writer, I need ways to enter the world of a story more quickly and under imperfect conditions.

One way to trigger my brain to return to a mood or a feeling is through music.

For pretty much an entire novel, I listened to the singer-songwriter Gregory Alan Isakov, whose atmospheric indie-folk music was the perfect un-distracting mood-setter. After a few days of hitting play on this shuffled mix, I found that the first chords brought me back to the space of the book even when I was writing for twenty minutes in a coffee shop or hiding in the bedroom while my husband managed pandemic homeschool (which, I would argue, was the fullest possible expression of imperfect conditions).

Key

Make a playlist of music that is not too distracting and that you can listen to a lot. I like for these songs to be in the same neighborhood vibe-wise, so that I can hit shuffle and enter the same musical space each day without getting bored. Every time you sit down to write, press play. Your brain will start to form a connection between the music and the writing.

Option A: Build the playlist specifically for the piece you are writing. Think about setting—if the story takes place in New York in 1996, maybe the playlist is built from music that might have been playing in coffee shops or clubs in Lower Manhattan that year. Maybe your work calls for holler-by-holler Kentucky bluegrass or Bay Area punk. Bring yourself to the place and space through your ears.

Option B: Build a playlist for each character. This is similar to the songwriting doorway. What does the character listen to? What music embodies them? What might they listen to in the car on the way home from a crappy date, or on a Sunday morning?

DOORWAY #78

Scent Story

Smell as Portal

I love the two weeks in spring when the lilacs bloom and everyone in my neighborhood—the old ladies, the long-distance runners, kids on their way to school—turns doglike, sniffing each purple-hazed bush. I walk a few steps, stop to put my face in the plume. I look for the darker blossoms, the freshly bloomed, searching for the richest scent. I grew up in New Mexico with lilacs, but then lived for most of my adult life in California, where the spring scents were more voluminous and lush, taking over whole blocks. Star jasmine is the smell of my early twenties, my robin's-egg-blue Vespa parked in a huge bank of white flowers. Orange blossoms bring me to a rainy February, a baby strapped to my chest and my other child pedaling his tiny tricycle to the corner store for samosas.

These days I live in Colorado and am back in the purple aura of lilacs. I have to slow down and press my nose into the lilac blooms to appreciate them. Though they are quieter and not as showy as the intoxication of star jasmine or lemon blossoms, every single breath is delicious, prompting a soft little "mmmm." The still life would be called *Woman Alone, Sighing with the Brief Pleasure of a Beloved Smell.*

Meanwhile, my companion, an actual dog, is building a historical record of the creatures of this route. Her nose can detect the size each animal was, its mood, whether it was dawn or dusk at the moment the scent was released. My nose says, "Lilacs! Spring!" Hers tells an entire story about who has passed this way over the last week.

Even with our low-tech noses, smell is perhaps the sense most instantly tied to memory. A whiff of something long forgotten brings us immediately back to a place or a moment, the recollection so strong it is almost present tense rather than remembered.

Key

Write a scent biography of a character. What are five or six smells that would trigger the strongest memories for them? Think of indoor smells—burning toast, laundry soap, lentils on the stove, a newborn baby's poop—or outdoor smells. Think of the scents of places or eras (I can still smell the shampoo we all fell for in the ninth grade).

Or write the scent landscape of your story. What are all the smells that make up this world?

Each of these scents is a key to enter the mind or emotions of your characters or the setting of your piece. The star jasmine is an entry, as is a whiff of city trash that reaches a garden-level apartment. Let the scent carry you there.

DOORWAY #79

Who Is Your Story To?

Writing for Your Perfect Reader

I've been thinking about audience a lot in the last few years. In his book *Craft in the Real World*, Matthew Salesses talks about the importance of getting to name your own audience or intended reader. The freedom to say, You, grouchy person who is complaining in workshop about not being able to picture the dish described in a story because it's from another culture—thanks, but the story isn't for you. Salesses, a Korean adoptee, writes about the choice to write for a Korean audience rather than a white audience. To write toward his origin rather than his upbringing. Not that anyone is excluded or disallowed, but a piece does not have to belong to everyone. Choosing your audience means choosing to write from a place of strength and confidence, rather than trying to explain everything to an outsider or skeptic.

Still, for me, the idea of "audience," no matter how loving, makes me clammy. I get nervous. I get anxious. I feel like I have to be good enough and smart enough and deserving enough, and I am immediately in doubt of all of that. When I think of "audience," I think of a huge army of ladies with the same hairdo standing in a chain bookstore, skimming my book and saying things like, "I don't get it—the cover made me think this would be a love story." Thinking of my audience makes me feel like I need to clean the toilet and bake something so the house smells good when people arrive.

Instead of asking myself, Who would read this?, I started asking, Who is this *to*? I realize this is not a grammatically correct sentence, but it feels like a different place to stand. It feels like I'm being invited to make a direct transmission, a wrapped present that's maybe got pretty gold paper and a big bow but what's inside is still private and safe. If I write a story to my friends who are always early readers, I've shut off the lights in that big theater, I've left the stage, and now the four of us are gathered in the back room with some peanuts and fizzy water and I'm giving them a thing I made. It feels like connecting a circuit—not to wire the city but to make one individual bulb turn on. The bulb that is my friend Marie, or Manuel, or Michael or Matt or Marisa (apparently I only trust people whose names begin with *M*). The bulb that is my husband. My literary agent, who is first a friend and reader before any of the business part.

Aside from moving me off the stage and quieting all those self-doubts, this way of thinking contains a profound truth. We do not reach readers en masse. Each person reads a book to him- or herself. One at a time. Sure, if Oprah's lightbulb goes on, then you suddenly have access to a whole lot of electricity, but it's not like turning on an entire grid at once. We reach one another individually, one at a damn time. It's a miracle, really, that I had an idea and I worked that idea through for years in my own head in my own house on my own street and somewhere, without my ever meeting the person, the circuit connects and a light flickers on in another head, another house, another street, another city. If I think of it that way—a current going to somewhere—I feel excited to fill that current with all the energy and electricity I have. I want to reach you. I want to be reached by you.

Key

Think about a reader or set of readers who make you feel more free. It might be about identifying who you are *not* writing to as much as who you are. Maybe you need to say to yourself that you are not writing this novel for your mother. Maybe you need to recognize, as Matthew Salesses did, that you want to write for people who are from your place, whatever that is to you. Maybe it's a certain person or group of people—friends, faceless but ideal readers, your teacher, your sisters.

Imagine the circuit your work creates between you and the people whose hands will eventually hold it. Imagine how powerful the charge is, how much light you can create together.

DOORWAY #80

Pretend to Try to Fix It

Be Your Own Small White Lie

Even several books in, with evidence that I can write a novel or an essay or a short story, I get psyched out when I open my laptop to write or revise a real live chapter. Right now? Today? But what if I don't know what should happen in this scene, or know how to decide which point of view will be most revealing? I am a small human person! Who put me in charge of this fictional universe, and when will they come tell me what should happen?!

This is the moment when I take a breath and say to myself, Yup, this is huge. Maybe impossible. Why don't we *pretend* to fix it?

I Save As and place my fingers on the keyboard. It's imaginary fixing, after all. Not only does the pressure come down in the land of make-believe, but the lie contains a truth: Writers don't do things because they *know* this tack will work. Writers try something to pretend it *might* work, to bring an imaginary choice into focus by playing it out on the page.

Key

Say to yourself, This is so hard! I don't know what to do! But as long as I'm sitting here, let's pretend to rewrite this chapter in present tense. Let's pretend to reorganize the scenes in reverse chronological order. Let's pretend to add some scenes of the main character at work.

This tiny white lie is your on-ramp—you aren't merging directly onto the rush-hour freeway, only climbing a gentle hill at twenty-five miles per hour.

DOORWAY #81

Be Kinder Than Necessary

To Yourself, to Your Work

Several years ago, I rented space in a coworking office to teach the still-pandemic, still-online Tin House Summer Workshop. I was spending time in my extended family's house on the East Coast. Every day, I left my kids and their cousins in the middle of morning cereal and sunscreen application and beach preparation and drove to this shared space where people I did not know were sitting at their desks, masked and working on laptops.

I taught the workshop from a private office with a view of the parking lot and a stand of oak trees. We had all been in the emergency of COVID for long enough to have grown weary and lonely. We wanted to be together even though we knew it was neither safe nor practical to risk a large gathering. My students that week were warm and generous with one another, and we laughed a lot. It was one of those quiet miracles—ten strangers reaching out toward one another on the page and through screens and finding real connection.

On the inside of the door of my workspace, someone had placed a bumper sticker with the words "BE KINDER THAN NECESSARY."

Not only kind, but kinder even than necessary. The writers in my workshop followed this directive without my ever prompting them. This sentence has stayed in my head in the years since.

Being alive is hard, especially if you're paying close attention. Writing a book is also hard and it will take years. It will require belief in yourself beyond what you have on hand. It will require returning to the project when you have no idea how to proceed. Writing a book will require friends and readers and people who don't think you're crazy for sitting alone for years on end to make something two-dimensional come to life. You will need so, so much kindness (from your people, from your readers). You are not going to make it without encouragement. Encouragement is essential, elemental. Generosity is not the same as praise. Being kind is not the same thing as being nice. One of the people from whom you'll need the most kindness when writing is yourself.

Last year I was struggling to find time to write. My job was full and complicated. There were always students who needed support and care and I had a long list of high-priority to-dos. I kept telling myself I would write after the semester got underway, after I finished reading MFA applications, after I hosted a big event, after thesis-defense season. The window never opened. I wrote a little but not in a sustained or satisfying way. Kindness did not move between me and my work.

This year, when I refigured my schedule, I put writing down first. Now, without exception, on Monday, Wednesday, and Friday, I write on my couch with my dog curled next to me before answering email, planning class, or grading, and on Tuesdays and Thursdays, which are my teaching days, I drive to one of a handful of cafés. I order a real breakfast and tea and

I sit there for ninety minutes and write. The food was wholly practical at first (if I ate in the late morning, then I could hold office hours right until class, thus maximizing the writing time), but the nourishment has been surprisingly important.

I look forward to my writing dates. This meal makes me feel so cared for. Cared for by myself, by the people I see every time I go into one of these restaurants, and by my writing, which is the reason I'm there. My work makes these sweet mornings what they are. I have prioritized writing in a lot of different ways over the years and have gotten plenty done, but this level of kindness is a new aspect of the relationship.

This year I picked up and finished a novel draft and I wrote the entirety of the book you are holding. It almost never felt like I was forcing work, but instead like I was going on a date with my projects, and both of us came out fuller and better cared for at the end.

Key

Logic is helpful when you're designing your practical goals and ambitions. We've considered writer math and using accelerated writing speed to get where you want to go. Now it's time to think about how you can create a reciprocal relationship of care so that your writing time leaves you feeling replenished and you actively want to return.

Maybe it's breakfast or coffee or cookies. Maybe it's knowing that you get to take a run after you write, or before. Maybe it's getting help cleaning the house so that you can write in a tidy space. Maybe it's as simple as looking forward to a hot cup of tea in the morning sun and thirty minutes when you don't have to attend to any of your other responsibilities. Naming the kindness is as important as what it contains. Reframe writing as a place of care where you value yourself and your time enough to make it lovely. Not only kind, but kinder than necessary.

DOORWAY #82

Do Something for Someone

Goodness Creates Goodness

In the dark of 2020, my friend Marie-Helene Bertino reached out to say that she was having trouble writing and had decided to take a purposeful break to see if she could help anyone else with their projects. "Do you need a reader?" she asked. Boy, did I. I was a couple of drafts into a novel and I had kept at it despite my kids being home suddenly and possibly forever. I had zero perspective, zero extra gusto, and a lot of questions.

"Are you serious?" I asked.

Within a few weeks she had read the novel and asked several questions that would guide the entire rest of the revision process. Marie let me back into my own world right at the moment when I was feeling outside of it (and outside of reality, for that matter). I will never forget this gift. She knows that I am standing by for the moment she needs the same kind of attention.

Feeling stuck is about not being able to make the energy move. Everything is simply *there*. Sometimes, the way to get the energy going again is by stirring the soup of the writing itself; sometimes we move the energy by making motions in another direction.

Key

It might be as simple as what goes around comes around, and maybe you will get back the very good thing you sent out. Probably the picture will be both more interesting and more complicated than that. I can tell you this, for sure: Being stuck feels bad and doing something nice for someone feels good, for you and for them. Acts of kindness can be writing-related or not. They can be tiny or large. They can be premeditated or impulsive. Every one of them is worth it.

- Write a fan letter to an author you love. Most writers have a website with an email address and/or a social media page where you can send them a DM.

- Pay for the drink of the person behind you in line at the coffee shop. Whatever you write that day will include the energy of this small kindness.

- Offer to read a draft for someone else.

- Post generous reviews for the last five things you read.

- Celebrate someone's good news.
- Drop by your bestie's house on a Tuesday for no reason with a pint of ice cream and a box of cones.
- Text six old friends to tell them you're thinking of them.
- Go walk dogs at the shelter.

If your writing can be the impetus for goodness, then no matter what else happens, you have that.

DOORWAY #83

Family Tree of Influence

Gathering the Magic, from Books, Movies, Songs, Art, and Nature

No question makes me more nervous than when I am asked about my influences, especially in public. Suddenly, I don't remember *any books* (have I ever read any books?!), and whatever I say will surely reveal how small-minded I am, how unimpressive my breadth of knowledge. The perfect recipe is something like a doorstop classic, an obscure novel translated from the Hungarian, a now-forgotten bestseller from the eighties that I discovered in a used bookstore in Paris, and a zine containing an otherwise unpublished story by the latest twenty-year-old wunderkind. Is that an honest answer? Definitely not.

I remember being afraid, early in my writing life, of showing my influences. As if I were supposed to be unique in the world, never before seen. In truth, I wrote for those first years powered by the bright heat of Sandra Cisneros. In college I was handed work by Yusef Komunyakaa, George Saunders, James Joyce, and Nella Larsen, and all of those became important to me. Even if I were to name four or five books that I have truly loved, the picture feels partial at best. In addition to reading the books my professors assigned in college, I stayed up late listening to Ben Harper while eating cheap pizza with people I had known for a matter of weeks and already felt transformed by. That must have had as much of an impact on my mind then as what I read. On weekends I gathered friends to go to Southern California beaches, to Disneyland, to wander around LA. Wherever we went, the beat of the car tires over the gray quilt of the 10 Freeway was constant. Who's to say that my poems in those years weren't influenced by that music? And that's only the 1998–99 snapshot.

These days I don't even try to name my influences as a writer. The list is too long and it only notes those I am conscious of. That being said, every project has family members, even early on, when that project is a tiny embryo or vat of primordial slush.

Having cousins and aunties and uncles is always a good thing, and none of us emerge out of deep space formed only by the force of our own explosion. Instead of the dread of trying to describe the fabric of my mind by way of six book titles that will make you think I'm smart or cool, an exercise I truly love is creating a constellation in which to place my current project.

Key

Build a network or a constellation of influence for your project with art, novels, poems, music, texture. Maybe you include a book or short story that has a longed-for sharp edge of humor or oddity and one that's got the lush moodiness your story reaches toward. Perhaps you include a novel steeped in place and a picture book with illustrations that remind you of the mood you're looking for. Maybe the song your dad listened to on repeat when you were in the third grade is in this project's sky. The texture of fake granite in a cheaply renovated kitchen, the smell of a natural foods store. The first chapter of *Moby-Dick*, which is all you've read of the book and all you plan to read. Maybe the choice *not* to read *Infinite Jest* is part of the constellation.

Place your project in this constellation. Let the sources be the cousins and aunties that hold your emerging star in space.

DOORWAY #84

A Modern *Hamlet*

Borrowing, Burning, and Coupling with Texts

We share a vast inheritance of literature. All of it belongs to all of us. With a library card or an excursion to a bookstore I can read (and by "read" I mean take into my mind and life) ancient Greek poems, comedic plays of the Velvet Revolution, a memoir of diamond mining in South Africa, a stack of modern Colombian novellas. What a crazy, lucky fact! We are literature billionaires!

Not only do I get to swim in this impossible beauty, but as a writer, I get to be in conversation with it. I've already created my constellation of influence, but sometimes I want to speak more directly to or against one piece. Sometimes I might lean on the walls erected by a piece of writing made three hundred years before I was born.

Key

You could invent the structure, the movement, of a story, but maybe William Shakespeare did it for you? What if you move all your own curiosity and questions into the house built by *Little Women* or *Frankenstein*? What stories did you grow up with? Is there one you want to move into and inhabit? Is there one you want to tear apart? Something that you love and resist at the same time? If your own weird genius had a baby with *Dracula*, what would that look like? (And please introduce me right away.)

You have the full range of possible relationships with any book ever written. You could retell an old story in modern times (see *Ten Things I Hate About You*/*The Taming of the Shrew*). You could center a supporting character (see *James* by Percival Everett/*Adventures of Huckleberry Finn* by Mark Twain). You could change the setting, change the message, upend every aspect of the piece, or focus on one.

DOORWAY #85

Radial Outline

Working Outward from the Middle to Find the Edge

When reading a story, we often have a clear sense of the origin and the landing place. Here is the sequence of events, one to the next, and here is where we are delivered to a moment of recognition and surprise. In our experience as readers, the order has been decided; it just *is*.

When writing a story, we have yet to make these choices, and they are choices that change not only the delivery but the meaning.

One of the most common conversations I have with students is about how to let the beginning wait. The beginning is the last thing I have a full understanding of because the beginning has to seed every living thing to come. The beginning has to make all else possible. It also has to scoop us up, to teach us how to live there. The idea that I would know how to do that when I'm starting to write a novel is absurd.

It's more common for me to have some sense of the ending, even if it's only an image. By the time I have a half draft or a full first draft, I often *still* don't know how to build the precision engine of the beginning. The ending is a loose version of itself at best. But I know at least one important thing about the middle. There is at least one solid stone in the middle on which to stand. From here, I can build outward, rotating or radiating until I find the edges and much of what they contain.

Key

Name the scene that you consider to be somewhere in the center of your story. It does not have to be on page 100 of 200, necessarily (though looking there can be a good place to start). Think about a hinge, a turn, a moment when a lot of feelings come together, a vortex. Write this in the center of a piece of blank paper. Now look at the scenes or moments before and after this and place those on the sides of the center dot. Keep working outward, placing labeled dots for each scene.

Part of the role of this exercise is to get off the one-lane highway of the linear. Use the full radius of the space, in addition to the center line. Perhaps scenes or moments in the past go below the midline and scenes casting ahead go above it.

Keep working in this way until you have come to the outside edges.

Seeing the array of scenes is a way to visualize the contents, and knowing the contents means you know what kind of container you have or need. The beginning and the end are the most container-ish sections of a story—they define what it is and what it is not, where the line between story and not-story is. Those edges can expand and contract. They can change shape. Let the contents push the container into its truest, best form.

DOORWAY #86

One Thing at a Time, Part 1

Pay Attention to Each Character

"Revision" is a word that means the universe. "Revision" might mean moving paragraphs around to create a stronger sense of tension; "revision" might mean going through an entire manuscript to make sure you haven't overused a metaphor; "revision" might mean turning the mother into a wolf or rewriting the second half as a prose poem or changing the entire backbone of a plot. When you say you're "revising," you could be talking about virtually anything.

When I return to the novel half draft I finished a few months ago, I will be holding a stack of pages that contain some scenes that work, some scenes that don't really fit in with the story as it evolved, characters who are partly present, a plot with some big decisions still to be made, and surely a mess of verb tenses and stylistic hullabaloo. YAY, OOF. How in the world am I supposed to begin the next draft?

I have a very hard time doing many things at once, and luckily productivity research backs up a more focused approach (multitasking is a way to fail at several things at once, a teacher used to say).

The first lesson is: Don't do it all at once.

There are thousands of decisions and ideas and possible tacks and you cannot attempt them simultaneously.

The second lesson is: Don't start by trying to revise the beginning.

I judged a first-novel contest a few years ago, and one thing I noticed was that a lot of the submissions had a very polished and well-conceived first fifty pages that felt deeply revised, probably after feedback from multiple readers. After this, the author simply needed to write the rest of the book, and I found the rest of the book to be less rich or fully formed than the first section. It makes sense that we'd get caught up in the first movement of a book over and over again—there it is, right at the beginning!

In order to see my way through from the beginning to the end without getting tangled up in the infinite decisions ahead, I separate threads—in this case, a thread is any element of the piece, from an individual character to a theme to a setting to an emotional texture—and work on one at a time. This doorway, which is about revising for character, is the first of several that bring you into that focused, beginning-to-end revision rhythm. They can be undertaken in any order, and you can use the theory to follow any inquiry relevant to your project.

Key

Pay attention to one character from page 1 to the last. Read the entire manuscript, but train your eye only on the protagonist or the antagonist, the mother or the brother. Take note of where they begin and where they land and how the events of the story contribute to their transformation (or lack thereof, you may find). Think about how prismatic their inner life is, how clearly their needs or questions come through, whether they keep hitting the same note. Before you begin to revise, map out the line or arc (or other shape) this character travels in your current draft and the line or arc you want to push them toward. Now spend a period of time paying attention only to this thread. By the end you will have coaxed this character up from the soil across the whole manuscript.

Then follow each of the other important characters from beginning to end.

In the last step, revise for the ensemble—the background actors who appear on the page, even if they aren't central.

DOORWAY #87

One Thing at a Time, Part 2

Thread by Thread

Having lived with and breathed into and loved and hated and cared about all the characters in a story, I can turn my attention to the next strand.

There are a thousand—more!—possibilities.

A whole draft, beginning to end, where all I'm paying attention to is the setting, the movement of time, the tension between language and subject, the color blue. I might read and revise for subtext only. Or I work on a draft where all I'm paying attention to is dialogue and making sure everyone's voice feels and sounds right, that every conversation is lit with friction. In my current novel there is a lot of swimming, so a draft I'll turn to at some point will be focused on all the swimming scenes: on the way the strokes are described, the emotional relationship the character has with the small local pool, then the fancy college pool, then the open ocean. I might look at sex and sexuality across the story, or anger or loss. Maybe I'll work on everyone's relationships with their bodies.

The lesson I learn and relearn is that the more times I walk the landscape of the novel, the more complex the world becomes. And I might never have noticed that anger is simmering but never bubbling over until I turn my focus to that and that alone. This method also keeps me moving at a real clip so I can see that I'm making progress, pushing movement, deepening and amplifying. I don't get caught in the swamp of trying to change or fix many things at once, which is both boring and impossible. Some one-stranded drafts might take me only a few days, and others might be longer efforts. There is no definition of a draft. I have a friend who considers each day's attempt a new draft, and he retitles them as such.

Key

Make a list of many possible elements to turn your attention toward. Start with bigger things so that you are tending to some story-wide questions or themes or ideas and thus building the backbone of the piece. As you move through, pay attention to the smaller, lacier elements. Follow-through is key—for each thread, work from the first page to the last page.

By giving yourself permission not to work on anything except body language and gesture, say, you relieve tremendous pressure. All the other parts get to sit quietly while you attend to one and only one inquiry.

Move through a dozen threads, at least. Keep the list alive by adding new ones when you notice them.

DOORWAY #88

One Thing at a Time, Part 3

Neon Paintbrush

After many single-thread drafts, and when the story has entered the realm of completeness, fullness, I embark on one of my favorite enterprises: a draft focused on the *bam-pow-zam*. Here, I am interested not in logic or cause and effect. I am not here for character arc, scene tightness, or any of the other many valuable drafts of the past. My whole job is to make sure that these pages light up. You could think of this as giving the book a nice head of bright highlights (if you're into blonds) or turning the stage lights on so the set pops to life or, as I do, coming in with a palette of neon paints. Depending on the story, this might be relatively subtle or very unsubtle—the difference between a single hot-pink dot and a full Jackson Pollock splatter array—but by the end of this draft, there should be a line, moment, or image on *every page* that pops or sparks. Something odd, funny, mean, noisy, bright. Something that prompts a corresponding electric spark in me.

Key

You aren't here to alter the fundamental tone of the work, like the artists who buy cheesy paintings in thrift stores and add a UFO or Bigfoot (though you certainly can take that approach). You are here to punch up and add dimension, to make sure you aren't leaving everything in shadow. There's real bravery in trusting a standout line, in arresting attention, in not being shy about a strong image or the delivery of a line of humor. A little eighties-aerobics-leotard green here, a little dazzling yellow there, a moment edged in hot pink—fortune favors the bold. Add a little bit of Hell Yeah. Turn the lights on and see what happens.

Part 4

Doorways Out: Later Drafts and Moving On

DOORWAY #89

A Night to Remember

Every Scene Is a Little Party

I have come a long way in my project. I have written and revised and toiled. I have worked and worked and worked. My very being is in these pages. I have zoomed out, reseen, mapped.

The time has come to send myself a party invitation.

In *The Art of Gathering*, Priya Parker talks about how, when hosting an event, people often think they want to be "chill" and not pressure guests to do particular things in particular ways. It's scary to be the conductor of a group of people! Parker argues that meaning and transformation are made by gathering with purpose and asking people to be part of a distinct moment together. A chill host doesn't ask you to get there at a specified time, doesn't ask you to say anything real, and the party, which might be perfectly nice, is forgettable. Writing a story is sort of like hosting a party. A chill writer keeps it loose—POV? Whatever! Setting? Here and there! Black hole? Uh, life! Characters? A couple of normal guys! Chill doesn't make strict decisions, and as a result, the story is forgettable.

So: Drop the chill and make it a party. Being awake to the world is sometimes easier when we are in new terrain. When it's an *event*.

I wrote a woolly mammoth into my novel partly because I really wanted to hang out with the goldendoodle of pachyderms. I wrote a story about the village in Romania where my grandmother was born because it was the only way I would be able to live for a while in that place and that time.

It's time to gather with purpose. Here we go.

Dear Book,
Let's meet on page 123 in the scene where the woolly mammoth is born and REALLY snuggle with it. Smell its skin, run our fingers through the fur, examine its eyelashes. No one has ever done this before ever, ever!!
Ramona

Dear Book,
You know the part where the two girls steal their mom's money and go out to eat? Can that be way more delicious and indulgent and feast-y? Can it also contain the essential nature of their shared love and anger? I thought so.
Ramona

Key

Is there a place in this piece of writing where you might expand or create a space of wonder or sheer delight or meaningful indulgence? A place where you can step all the way into your role as orchestrator and turn a moment (every moment is a little party!) into a fully articulated container for what matters most right then? Look at places where the decision-maker in you was fatigued in earlier drafts and you now feel ready to drop the cloak of chill. Set an arrival time, a dress code, make everyone reveal their most embarrassing childhood memory, and watch as your decisive, fullhearted care sets real magic in motion.

DOORWAY #90

Get Flat

To Solve a Puzzle, Lie on the Dang Floor

Sometimes what's needed to push past a barrier is to keep pressing onward, to stay in the chair. Sometimes what's needed is to change your external landscape, to move your body. The novelist Rebecca Makkai writes in her Substack that, for a long time, she thought the bathroom at her favorite Starbucks was a vortex of good ideas, but then she realized that the good ideas came as a result of standing up from her laptop and walking twenty steps. You already know how I feel about walks. A hot shower can be highly generative.

Not all revelation-friendly moves need to raise your heart rate. Before my editor, Masie Cochran, began working remotely, she was known for the spot by the office supply closet where she would lie on the floor when she was stuck on an edit. Everyone in the Tin House office knew when Masie was struggling to figure out a puzzle because she would leave her desk and go flat for as long as she needed before things clicked into place. She reasons that the mild discomfort of lying on a hard surface makes her brain act like it's in a tiny emergency and kicks it into action.

Many meditation practices include some mild to moderate physical discomfort—hours sitting straight-backed on the floor or on a small, hard cushion. To press the mind out of its comfortable, worn paths, the body needs to do the same.

Key

Stand up from your chair, stretch, and go lie on your back on the floor. Do not bring a pillow. Close your eyes, if you want to. Stay for at least ten minutes (this might feel long, which is a good thing!) to allow the altered perspective to work on your brain and body.

DOORWAY #91

Read Aloud

Listen to Your Own Work

One of the many challenges of being deep in a piece of work is that it becomes harder and harder to see what it even is. You know when you repeat a word enough times that it turns into gobbledygook in your mouth and no longer means anything? Writing a novel is like that, only with ninety thousand nonsense words, ten characters, thirty subplots, seven hundred scenes, and a giant cause-and-effect machine that feels like it's made out of macaroni noodles, baseball gloves, fresh daisies, hot glue, and a wild rat that keeps eating everything. Not to put too fine a point on it.

Being able to simply perceive what you have made is a true challenge.

When I was in graduate school, we each got a turn to read from our work out in the world somewhere. My turn took place at a bookstore in arguably the bougiest mall in Southern California (home of many bougie malls). While women with fat collagen lips shopped for teeny Louis Vuitton purses, velvet tracksuits, and diamond bracelets, I stood up between stacks of nonfiction in front of my friends with printed pages in my hand that I thought I understood. As I read aloud, I heard every off word, every line that went on a breath too long, every missing beat. When I was done, I borrowed a pen from the checkout counter and scribbled all over the manuscript. I had discovered one of the most powerful tools: my own voice. To celebrate my first reading as a fiction writer and all the discoveries that came from hearing the story aloud, I bought a giant bag of kettle corn and walked around the mall feeling richer than all those real housewives of Orange County with their shopping bags full of luxury.

Key

The starter home of reading aloud is to do this in a private place where the only ears in the room are your own. This is surprisingly effective. I read every single story I write aloud a bunch of times, once in each draft. I always, always hear things I didn't see.

Step two is to invite one other person in. Your partner, a friend, another writer. Your dog would probably really enjoy this exercise, even though she might sleep through it.

When you're ready, sign up for an open mic or assemble other writers for a group reading. I guarantee that you will hear the work differently in each of these settings. You will be able to see what you have, no matter how many times you've looked at it.

DOORWAY #92

Robot Read Aloud

The Value of Hearing Your Words in the Voice of an AI

I have read my story aloud to myself, to my dog, to a room full of others. Because I'm the one reading it, the sentences come out the way I hear them in my head. For the next step of defamiliarization, it's time to up the ante.

Nonfiction author Lacy M. Johnson tells me that she puts the piece in a font she finds "gross," which makes her want to make changes.

When Tommy Orange was writing his novel *There There*, a finalist for the Pulitzer Prize, he downloaded an early version of an AI reader and had the robot read his pages to him. The voice was entirely unhuman and he told the MFA students at the Institute of American Indian Arts that he found this ideal—like Lacy's gross font, the machine voice allowed Tommy to hear everything that might be better. It took away any smoothness, any expected intonation or rhythm. It revealed what was not yet right.

Key

Choose a text-to-voice AI reader (there are lots in the App Store and online) and have it read your work back to you, one section at a time. Take it slow. Start with a page, revise that page, then continue. Allow the discomfort of the robot delivery to open you to changes you had not considered before.

For a double whammy, change the font so that you are both seeing and hearing something unfamiliar.

Not only will you resee the piece and make meaningful changes, but the relief of putting it back in your comfy font and reading it in your human voice will feel like coming home after a camping trip. A real bed! A hot shower! Welcome back.

DOORWAY #93

Scout Badges

A Story Worth Sending Out, a Draft Achieved, a Risk Taken

Publication is one and only one measure of success, and to hold this as the ultimate meaning-maker in our writerly lives is so, so limiting. I cannot control the editorial decisions at *The New Yorker*, but I can control whether I have a story good enough to send to them. I cannot know the future of a novel, but I can make a commitment to write every day until I have a draft. I was talking to a friend recently who described the feeling of wanting to turtle into her writing and really, really listen to what it wanted to become, rather than write toward a marketplace or external measure of success. She's making a real, meaningful choice when she values her voice, her art, and I wanted to give her a Scout badge that said "Chose the Turtle Shell."

It made me realize how many dozens (hundreds? thousands?) of small and big choices we make that deserve real and sustained appreciation and places of honor on our little green Writer Scout vests.

Some recent Scout badges I have proudly earned: Took a day off writing to play in the snow with my kids! Got to Doorway #93 of 101!! Sent a story to a fancy friend who was guest editing a fancy journal, even though that was so scary! Dared to start a new novel!!!! Showed the eff up to write on Tuesday! Thought about my book while washing dishes! Wrote in my detail journal every day!

These are not stopovers on the way to "real" success. These are not sidebars or consolation prizes. This *is* the real work, and we deserve badges of honor for each and every one.

Key

Make it a practice to see and name the things that make you proud. Small victories are very important here! Bestow on yourself badges upon badges, and mean it. Fill that writerly vest up with glory.

DOORWAY #94

Art Lives Its Own Life

Release What You Made into the Wild

Last fall I taught at a writing conference on the California coast, and though I was very glad to be there, I arrived feeling tired and depleted. My regular teaching job had been hard, and students needed a lot from me. The thing that made me feel smallest was that I was supposed to read from my work and I felt like I didn't have anything new and had not had anything new for ages. I was working on a novel and none of it was even slightly ready for the world. The only recent piece was a story that had been narrowly rejected by a glossy magazine, and even though I had done my best to celebrate that as a win ("Narrowly Rejected by a Glossy Magazine" Scout badge!), I had let the pass color my view of the story. Still, I had the front desk print the pages and I read them to a room full of writers. After, one of the students in my workshop came up to me and said, "That story was about me. Not me, but me. I needed that." I had not known this woman before. I had not known her while I was writing the story, but it felt so clear, so absolutely true, that I had written it for her. Nothing else about the story will ever matter as much as that moment. One writer, one reader, and a story-bridge between us—what a true, true miracle.

Every book I have published feels like an animal I've set free into the wild. It will eat and drink and wander beyond the yard where it was raised. The life it leads is no longer about me, and this sets me free, too.

I think of the ways I have been reached by a piece of art, the way seeing Botticelli's paintings when I was fifteen opened me to the world; the way short stories have freed me over and over again. The way they live in my very cells. That's it, that's the biggest and most real it gets.

Key

When you have traveled with a piece of writing up and around, back and forth, through drafts and revisions and retypings, the story has work to do beyond your desk, beyond your control. It belongs to someone, somewhere.

Send the piece to a few journals. Send it to a few friends or beloveds. Read it aloud to a group of strangers. Share it with your writing group.

In order for work to meet the person or people it was made for, even if you as the maker never see that connection, you must let it go. You have to release it into the wild, into the wilderness. It will live a life beyond you. You were altered by the making of the story, and others may be altered by the reading of it. Trust that it will find its way.

DOORWAY #95

Take a Break, but Write Something New

Matter Begets Matter

When I was nineteen, I babysat for a six-month-old baby. I hadn't spent much time with babies, and other than handing her toys that she chewed on and smiling and chatting back to her babble, I had no tricks. One of my jobs was to get her to go to sleep, and this was a job I failed at. I put her in the stroller, I bounced her on my hip, I laid her in her crib, but she stayed persistently and very much awake. Her parents came home from their date at 10 p.m., and I could see their good mood fade when they saw that their precious daughter was not lights-out but very much lights-on, fussy, and in need of care.

"I'm sorry," I said. "Hopefully she'll sleep in in the morning?"

The mom gave me a cold stare and said, "That's not how it works. Sleep makes sleep."

This rule works for a lot of things (love builds love, good habits breed more good habits), and it definitely works for writing.

Sometimes I take full breaks where I write nothing. This is important for rest and play and time spent doing the other things that matter to me (eating pie with my family, lying in the shade on a beach, walking fifteen miles around a city, sliding down a mountain on two slick sticks, looking at art, knitting while watching basketball with my kids, baking scones, calling my mom, petting the dog, and on forever and ever, wow, what luck to be alive).

When it's not time for a *break* break, but it is time for me to look away from the thing at which I have been staring for some time, I am a big fan of writing something else. My first four books were pairs of twins—a novel and story collection in each fraternal set. This was far from accidental. The novels were so unknown and unknowable over such a very long time, and I could not predict whether they would turn into real living books or if they would whirl around like a cast spell that would fizzle into sparks but never transform a feather into a white rabbit or a white rabbit into a lollipop. It's hard to live with that level of unknown every day, hour after hour, month after month, year after year.

Enter the short story as life preserver. Writing a story was joyfully straightforward compared with writing a novel. I had confidence that I could conjure ten or fifteen or twenty pages and that within this I could make something interesting occur. I wrote a story about people who grow new arms when they fall in love and a kid whose parents try to cremate their dead cat in the yard. I went wherever I felt like going. It was, dare I say, fun. It was also sort of restful by virtue of being so much less existentially terrifying than those early long-form experiments. If novel writing (at least for those first books—I don't feel quite the same way now) was like swimming alone in the middle of the depthless ocean with nothing but a pair of too-small water wings, then hanging out with those stories felt like floating down a gentle river on an inner tube while holding a cold soda in a koozie.

The real surprise was that when I went back to the novel after my rest on the story swan, I had new energy and ideas for the longer project. As if the story had taught me what the novel needed. As if the story had packed me a lunch for the novel-writing journey ahead. What I know is that I was a better novelist after having worked on short fiction. I was also less tired, less dispirited, and more excited to flap my arms and put my head under the water and see what was swimming in the big ocean.

Key

> When your eyes are crossing and you feel like you want to bury your project in the bottom of a deep hole or at least hire a (competent, hopefully) babysitter so you can have a night off, open a new document or dig through the files for something playful. This is a perfect time for a big "what if," or an irreverent "eff it, I'm just going to . . ."
>
> Get out your heart-shaped sunnies, pop open a bubbly water and a bag of potato chips, and board your swan floatie. Curiosity makes curiosity. Writing makes writing. Float on, little sailor.

DOORWAY #96

Write a Query Letter

When It's Time to Introduce Yourself and Your Work, Who Will You Be?

Most of the time I think the specter of publishing haunts writers in a bad way. At conferences the ask-an-agent panels are always crowded, and while the questions new writers have are all perfectly valid (What do you look for in a novel? What pitfalls should I avoid? How can I build my platform?), none of them really matter unless the writer has lived with, and been eaten alive by, and fallen in love with, and returned a thousand times to a book that will make the agent in question miss her stop on the subway and/or forget her own name. That's an exaggeration, but only a small one. These people read for a living, and pretty good or even good-good is not going to be enough.

The writing, the manuscript, is *it*. Writing a query letter to pitch your work to an potential agent or editor is infinitely, absurdly easier than writing a novel. As in the difference between making toast and inventing the internal combustion engine, checking the mail and raising a child, tying your shoe and starting a new life in rural Tajikistan. I could go on.

These are the thoughts that came to mind when my third-year MFA students asked if I would meet with them for a biweekly informal professionalization club. "PAY ATTENTION TO YOUR THESIS!!!" I wanted to say. And I did say that, except not in all caps, and I also agreed to try this idea out.

So we met every other week for a semester, and we talked about how to read your work in public and where to look for summer writing conferences and residencies and how to throw together a DIY writing retreat. We also talked about query letters, which made me nervous because I worried that their art-minds would be taken over by the capitalist venture of trying to sell something before they knew what that thing even was. But a weird thing happened: The query writing was revelatory and meaningful.

No one in the group was at all ready to send anything to a real-life agent, so all my fears about premature concern with the marketplace turned out to be null. Every person who described their manuscript in a query letter draft said a version of "So *that's* what I'm trying to write." This small, concise, outward-facing articulation of what had so far been an inward-facing project allowed the writers to see what they had made. It also revealed the places where the work was not yet what they wanted it to become.

Another productive pleasure was when they wrote the bio that they wanted to grow into by the time the book was ready to send out. This bio was not allowed to be total fantasy—seventeen Pushcart Prizes, a story in *Best American*, the Rome Prize, and a MacArthur. Instead, they were to imagine real things the version of them in three, five, or seven years might have done. Where they wanted to conduct research, partnerships they might seek, conferences to attend. This bio became a near-future author character, and the writers were invited to begin to inhabit this version of themselves.

I still firmly believe that 99.9 percent of our effort should go to the work itself, but I am now a believer in the early query letter as imaginative practice.

Key

A query letter typically has two main parts:

1. A description of the book that captures both its content and its spirit. This should be written with energy and heart. Instead of trying to convince an outside skeptic (which feels yucky and triggers all manner of self-doubt), write toward a figure who loves exactly what you're doing and wants it to succeed.

2. A biography of you, the author, that contains all the reasons why you are the perfect person to write this book. Imagine this is you a few years hence—who do you want that person to be? What partnerships do you want to have formed? What research would you like to have done? What residencies or fellowships would you be proud to have applied to?

DOORWAY #97

Dear Writing

Pay Attention to What You Love

My writing is a relationship. It's a relationship with words and a way of seeing, with a quality of attention I pay to the world around me. Each piece is a relationship in a more specific way. Each character, each question. The relationship changes all the time, like the living thing it is.

In my early career I felt like a poet who wrote short fiction. If there had been a more voracious market for short story collections, I doubt I ever would have tried to write a novel. The idea of writing a novel felt like taking all my care for the line and the image and the paragraph and forcing it through a pasta press a thousand times until both the manuscript and I came out squashed and elongated. It did not turn out to feel quite like that, luckily. Still, the pain-to-pleasure ratio was in my favor with short stories.

They say you date a story and marry a novel. As marriages go, five or eight or ten years is short, but the depth of commitment rings true.

Now, after two collections of stories and three novels, I have come to love the relationship with those long works, which braid and twist into my own life. I think about a character while washing the dishes; an overheard piece of a conversation in the grocery store unlocks a scene. I get to live two lives at the same time. For years, I visit places in my pages—an Icelandic fjord, a Romanian birch forest, a sailboat in the middle of the Atlantic, a version of the attic in my aunt's house in Berkeley.

The more I think of writing a piece as a relationship I get to have, the less I worry about the perpetual march toward doneness and the less I feel the pain of not yet having arrived there. I am here, in the making. I am living in this place, with these people. The puzzle of form and shape and architecture is often a pleasurable one, ever evolving.

As in a marriage, it helps to keep choosing your partner over and over. Every human and every manuscript has inscrutable, irritating qualities. Sometimes the fact that the dishwasher didn't get unloaded seems louder than the fact that my husband cooked everyone breakfast. Sometimes, a squishy, boring character is all I notice, when there are five others who are popping to life. To stay in it, it helps to name what I love, what I admire. It helps to say thank you. It helps to remember that I want to be in this relationship, that I am here, with this work at this time, on purpose.

Key

Think about and name all the things you like or love or are engaged by in the piece of work at hand. The image of the plum tree about to bloom; the way the brother and sister seem to exist in their own world; the way sound works in the scene with the minor kitchen fire; the mother's sass; the way the piece makes a space for your anger. Allow humility and self-doubt to sit on the couch and play a round of gin—this assignment is the appreciation show and there's no room for anything else. You can write this as a letter to the piece itself, if you want. Write it as a list. Write it as a small essay.

You have kept coming back. Kept listening. Kept typing or scribbling. This is a world you have lived in. Name its beauty. Offer thanks for the gifts it brings.

DOORWAY #98

Behind the Scenes

What Happened to You While You Were Writing the Story

When I was in high school, I lived in Santa Fe, New Mexico, and it was before the internet so the world, the big actual world, came to me through tiny little portholes. I read magazines at the café that sold *Interview* and *Details* and *Vogue*. Sometimes a film crew cleared us out of the plaza (plaza rats, we were called) to shoot a scene for a movie. My friends Melissa and Heather and I would wander the fluorescent aisles of the music store, flipping the plastic pages of CDs: Tupac, Biggie Smalls, Radiohead, Smashing Pumpkins. The CD was still new—my first music was all on cassette tape and much of it was captured by listening to KISS 97.3 until my favorite song came on, then quickly pressing record on the tape player. For years, most of my music was absent the first five seconds.

My best source for information about culture was watching MTV and VH1. My favorite show was *Behind the Music*, in which famous people did not-famous things (celebrities, as we are always glad to learn, are just like us). I loved to hear a song I knew (caught like a firefly off the radio) in its early beginnings, plucked on guitar strings by a singer who did not yet know what she was trying to sing. It was such a private, simple joy, to quietly cheer from my couch: That's going to turn out to be so good.

The musicians ate chips and rode on their tour buses. There were roadies and groupies. One time my friends and I were at the motel pool where you could pay to swim for the day and there was a band there, on tour from Nashville, and we made friends and hung out in the sun and talked about how tired they were of road food. It was clear they were thrilled that this crappy motel had come with a side of local girls who didn't care that a band put up in these accommodations was probably small beans. They left the next day for El Paso or Flagstaff or Denver and I don't remember the name of the band, but in my head there's a scene in *Behind the Music* of all of us eating nachos and splashing one another with electric-blue pool water. Maybe a song came out of that day—I'll never know. Here I am, almost thirty years later, writing about it.

I love all the little twisty ties between my fiction and my life. I love that the attic where the teenage daughters in *The Last Animal* hang out is based on the attic at my aunt Sue's house. This is also the attic in Danzy Senna's novel *Caucasia* (my aunt has shared her home with a lot of different people over the years, and who knows how many pieces of art are twisty tied to that shingled old structure). I love how absolutely certain I feel that my daughter helped me write *Sons and Daughters of Ease and Plenty* in utero, as I (we!) sat in the same café chair every day for six months pressing that world into being while she turned from tadpole to human. Even though these details are not in the books, are invisible from the outside, they are part of the universe of the stories. They matter to me. They remind me of all the worlds I have occupied, all the selves I have been in the making.

Key

Write your own *Behind the Music*. Honor the weeks or months or years you have spent with this work by documenting what happened to you during its creation. Pay attention to the way in which writing has connected you to the world—the places where you wrote, the mornings you saw because you were up early at your desk, the friendships you formed because of this effort. Think about the choices you didn't yet know would matter and the way early instincts led you toward or away from the place you now land. This is the story of the story, and it has meaning no matter what happens next with the work itself. Art has connected you to your life and your life has connected you to your art. Look at all those little ties, twisted tight.

DOORWAY #99

Throw an Actual Party

Claim Joy, Bring Cookies

Once, in a Q and A after a reading, I heard someone ask Susan Orlean what advice she would give to her younger self and she said, "Throw a party. For everything." At the time I thought that I would absolutely follow this advice, but to be completely honest, I have kind of a hard time with this one. I don't like attention on me, and I don't want people to think that *I* think something is a bigger deal than it is. I'm working on this. Everything is exactly as big a deal as it is, which is to say that everything matters and the scale of its mattering is not the important calculation of the moment. The important calculation of the moment is: Would it be more fun to have cake or key lime pie? In what way and with which beloveds do I want to mark this happy occasion?

When I finished the first draft (that crazy, wild-eyed, nearly unreadable first draft written over six weeks) of my first novel, I took my husband out for sushi and a movie. I remember that evening in such sharp, bright detail. I was so, so proud that I had arrived at that point. That I had kept writing day after day, ten new pages every time I closed my laptop. I had 250-some pages that definitely existed. I now know how very many drafts would follow, and how tremendous the effort ahead would be, but I'm happy that I stopped there to celebrate. That was an absolutely terrific milestone.

One of the very best parts about being a working writer is celebrating the happinesses of my writer friends. I love this, unequivocally and with my whole heart. I always want to be invited to their book launches, their draft-completion parties, their starting-a-new-thing parties. When someone else opens their door so that I can high-five them, it makes a little more space in me to feel the pleasure of my own efforts. When I doubt that I deserve the party, doubt whether this milestone is enough, I remember this.

Key

> It's easy to think that whatever good thing you're experiencing is small in comparison to a cooler, better thing down the road, or the thing your friend Jeff got. There's only one way to get this right, and that is to celebrate all of it. Things you officially deserve to make a big deal of: Sending a story out for the first time! Getting something published in a tiny journal that no one has heard of! Getting something published in a big journal that at least fifty people have heard of! Getting an agent! Deciding to skip getting an agent and self-publish your memoir! Writing the acknowledgments for a book you've been working on for ten years! Letting something go that is no longer the thing that you want to be working on! Finishing another draft! And another! Starting something new!

You've given yourself a badge, and now you get to gather your partner or your parents or your closest friends or your colleagues or your whole damn town. Be proud and accept high fives and hugs. Dance about it. Pop open something with bubbles and clink glasses and mark the moment. One of many. Small, medium, large, yes yes yes.

DOORWAY #100

The Envy Recycler

Toss It, Make It into Something Better

The glittery good fortune of another writer's life viewed on or off the internet is an infinite candy box of potential heartache. One friend got a six-figure advance on their first book; one friend signed with *the* literary agent; one friend got a story published in *The Paris Review*; one friend got a celebrity book club endorsement; one friend posted a selfie with Ernest Hemingway (okay, not exactly, but it felt like that).

These are all real, true things that happened, and when they did, a little weight of jealousy dropped to the bottom of my throat.

The longer I have written, the more I have seen all that surrounds these lovely little blips of fortune. The pressure of a big advance on a first book; the way the best agent is an advocate, not only a name on the email; the way a glossy publication fades with time; the smallness of sales as a metric for meaning; the way even the sexiest, coolest person is only a person. Most every one of us will at some point need help in the bathroom. We are, as my friend Laleh Khadivi always reminds me, monkeys. Every life is populated by losses, even if you can't see them.

On a regular basis, I run the phrase "comparison is the thief of joy" through my fingers like a set of beads.

Instead of only trying to squash envy, I prefer to recycle it. Jealousy is a powerful feeling, and I don't want to waste power.

First, turn the envy into idealized desire: "I'm jealous that P got a story in *The Paris Review*" becomes "I want to have a story in *The Paris Review*."

Second, turn idealized desire into ambitious desire: "I want to have a story in *The Paris Review*" becomes "I want to write a story good enough to send to *The Paris Review*."

Third, turn ambitious desire into firelit effort: "I want to write a story good enough to send to *The Paris Review*" becomes "I am going to work on a story every day for the next three months, at which time I'll send it to someone I trust for feedback. Then I'll repeat these steps until I feel good, better, best about the story, and off it will go."

In this way, envy turns me back to my own work but with new fuel. Desire is part of making art: desire to connect, to move someone, to be heard. Desire to be seen by my peers. To be part of the conversation. I am greedy with my desire to do my best work, to try hard.

The envy recycler works in a way I had not anticipated: The more I see how hard everyone is working, how much the efforts of others sustain me via the work they write (not the jealousy of it, but the actual writing that I love to read), the more I am also greedy on their behalf. Greedy for all the books and essays and stories and poems written by people I love or don't know, greedy for their good news, for their overjoyed texts when the work crests the edge and spills over.

Key

When envy lands on you, run it through the recycler. Turn jealousy into idealized desire, then ambitious desire, then effort.

The only reason to be jealous is if there were a scarcity of possible good news, but there isn't. There is room for all of us to do our best work and find our appreciators. Be part of the chorus of celebration and praise. For your own efforts, for the efforts of others. Let that desire be the pulse that pushes you onward.

DOORWAY #101

Begin Anywhere

(Again)

I was in New York on the day my first novel sold. I was standing on Broadway and Eighty-Sixth when my agent called, and I leapt into the air. It was such a huge and wild feeling, bigger than the space of my body, bigger than the space of the entire city. I shouted and yelped. It was New York, so no one even gave me a second glance.

Here's what surprised me: When I hung up, I thought, Now I get to do it again. This was the best news of all. I would soon be able to burrow back down into my own way of seeing, into my own mind and heart and life, and find another story in which to live. I had come to the end, to the high mountain peak of accomplishment, and what mattered to me most was that I would soon be in a new valley.

We talk all the time as if the finished product were the goal. We are revising because we want to get to the end, and I'm not going to tell you that the end isn't nice. It's pretty up there, and there might even be four or five other people to give me a high five. Sometimes one of them has access to a printing press. But that little hilltop of accomplishment is nothing compared to the lands we inhabit while we are writing. The making and remaking, the circling of that black hole, those are the high peaks and deserts and all the oceans and forests and outer space, and my mother is there and so is my childhood dog, and if I want my ancestors ten generations back to be there, then they are, and if I want a lovelorn Cyclops to be there, or a mummified egg or a herd of wild horses, then they are. I'm telling you true, writing *is* the prize.

I want you to finish a project and hold it in your hands. But here's what I know: When you get there, after the high fives and a cocktail, everyone else will go home and all you'll be left with is a chair and a desk, your own mind, and a thousand, million doorways. And it will be the most beautiful thing in the world.

Key

This time I'm handing you a big brass key ring with nothing on it. Start a practice of writing down the things you know about your own process, your hard-earned wisdom and instinctive genius. Clip those keys onto the ring and keep them with you. You have written your way here and you will write your way onward. Pay attention, trust yourself, and give everything away to your pages.

Acknowledgments

Greatest thanks to Masie Cochran for warm hands and sharp eyes and for making a perfect home for this project. To Molly Stern, Becky Kraemer, Julia Talley, Tiffani Ren, Laura Schmitt, and everyone at Tin House/Zando for the many kinds of care this book received. To my ever-wonderful agent, PJ Mark.

To the Marty Bucco Award for Creative Teaching and Scholarship at Colorado State University for early support.

To the MFA programs at the Institute of American Indian Arts, Bennington, and CSU, and to conferences like Writing by Writers, the Bread Loaf Environmental Writers' Conference, the Tin House Workshop, Writing Workshops Paris, and the Community of Writers, where parts of this book began as craft talks and conversations.

Most especially and exuberantly, thank you to everyone with whom I have ever shared a classroom or space of learning—my teachers, colleagues, and students—it's an honor to learn with you. When I started out, I thought about the things *I* wanted to write, but it turns out that the purest happiness has come from glimpsing *your* early work, watching that work grow into itself, and seeing it matter in the world. Thank you, thank you, thank you, for letting me be part of your practice, your words, and your lives.

BEOWULF SHEEHAN

Ramona Ausubel is the author of five books, most recently *The Last Animal*, which was a national bestseller, received the National Book Foundation Science + Literature Prize and was a Barnes & Noble book of the month. Her previous books are *Awayland: Stories*, *Sons and Daughters of Ease and Plenty*, *A Guide to Being Born: Stories*, and *No One Is Here Except All of Us*. She has received the PEN/USA Fiction Award, the VCU Cabell First Novelist Award and has been a finalist for both the California and Colorado Book Awards and the New York Public Library Young Lions Fiction Award. Her work has been published in *The New Yorker*, *The New York Times*, *The Paris Review Daily*, *One Story*, *Tin House*, *Oxford American*, *Ploughshares*, and elsewhere. She is a professor at Colorado State University and has taught in the Bennington Writing Seminars, Tin House Workshop, Writing by Writers, Community of Writers, Bread Loaf Environmental Writers' Conference, and Writing Workshops Paris. She lives in Boulder, Colorado, with her family.